JEREMIAH

COURAGE
IN A
CANCEL
CULTURE

JEREMIAH

COURAGE IN A CANCEL CULTURE

A 40-Day Journey through the Word

with Tony Perkins

FIDELIS PUBLISHING ®

ISBN: 9781956454369
ISBN (eBook): 9781956454376

Jeremiah: Courage in a Cancel Culture
A Stand on the Word Study Guide

Cover design by Diana Lawrence
Interior layout design by Lisa Parnell
Copyedited by Lisa Parnell

Order at www.faithfultext.com for a significant discount. Email info@fidelis publishing.com to inquire about bulk purchase discounts.

Fidelis Publishing, LLC Sterling, VA•Nashville, TN fidelispublishing.com

Contents

Introduction

Welcome to *Jeremiah: Courage in a Cancel Culture, A 40-Day Journey through the Word.* With this Stand on the Word Study Guide, we will find that Jeremiah was the prophet the culture couldn't cancel. Now, why was Jeremiah the prophet they couldn't cancel? Well, it wasn't for lack of trying, which we'll see as we make our way through the book of Jeremiah. But as hard as they tried—they de-platformed him; they banned him from speaking at the temple, which was the center of communications in that day; they opposed him, jailed him, and even ripped up and burned his prophecies—yet Jeremiah continued to deliver the words of the Lord passionately and faithfully. In fact, we're reading it more than 2,500 years later. But before we get into the first chapter, let's consider some background to the book of Jeremiah.

Background

Jeremiah was the son of a priest from the small town of Anathoth in Judah. God called him to be a prophet around the age of twenty during the reign of King Josiah. Josiah was the last godly king of Judah. His rule came on the heels of the wicked King Manasseh, his grandfather. But a revival of sorts and reform occurred during Josiah's reign. Jeremiah had a good relationship with King Josiah, but after Josiah's death, it was downhill for the prophet's public ministry. The reason? Both those in authority and the people in general opposed Jeremiah because of the words of judgment God gave him to speak to their sin and apostasy. Consequently, Jeremiah's message weighed upon him emotionally. So it is not surprising that many refer to him as the "weeping prophet." Jeremiah's ministry began around 627 BC, and it continued into the period of Babylonian captivity after the destruction of Jerusalem took place in 586 BC. He was taken unwillingly to Egypt by a group of Jewish refugees, where he died sometime around 582 BC.

While most of his message was one of judgment, Jeremiah's prophecy contains some of the most hope-filled and encouraging words in all the Bible. In fact, Jeremiah 29:11 has become a favorite social media post for many believers: "For I know the thoughts that I think toward you, says the LORD, thoughts of peace and not of evil, to give you a future and a hope." Then there are verses 12–13: "Then you will call upon Me and go and pray to Me, and I will listen to you. And you will seek Me and find Me, when you search for Me with all your heart." Perhaps the high point of the prophecy is God's promise of a new covenant, which would be God's means of restoring His broken relationship with His people (see 31:31–34). Through it, God promised to place His law within them, writing it on their hearts of flesh rather than on tablets of stone. Also, rather than looking to a fixed location like the temple for meeting with God, He promised through Jeremiah that His people would know Him directly. Obviously, that personal relationship with God was made possible through the messianic "branch" or son of David whom Jeremiah prophesied about (23:5–6; 33:15–16), ultimately fulfilled in Jesus Christ. All of that and more is in the book of Jeremiah.

How to Get the Most from the Study Guide

While the study guide offers spiritual insights and applications, the real impact comes from the words of Scripture, which is the Word of God. Please read the selected text for the day in your own Bible. God's Word is living and active (Heb. 4:12). The Spirit of God uses His Word to change your life. Nothing else can do that. So before reading the daily commentary, read God's Word! In fact, here are five habits to cultivate as you approach God's Word each day.

1. ***Read it through:*** Don't skip around. Read the entire selection of Scripture. If you are pressed for time, please read the Bible before you read the study guide notes. So read it through.
2. ***Think it over:*** Meditate on it. Let it marinate in your mind. If you can, take notes. We provide a notes page at the end of each day. Think it over.
3. ***Pray it in:*** Personalize the Scripture. Turn the verse that speaks to you into a prayer, and pray it into your life. Ask God what you need to do in response. That leads us to the next habit.
4. ***Live it out:*** Consider ways to apply what God is revealing to you, ways you can obey Him. Put His word into practice. Make it a part of who you are, how you think, how you speak, and behave toward God and other people. In other words, take God's Word and live it out.
5. ***Pass it on.*** Don't keep it to yourself. There are people in your life who need the same truth God has spoken to you in His Word. Share it. Pass it on.

About Stand on the Word

Stand on the Word is a ministry of Family Research Council, whose mission is to advance faith, family, and freedom in public policy and the culture from a biblical worldview. The purpose of Stand on the Word is to lay the foundation for a biblical worldview through daily reading and engaging of God's Word. For the daily journey, we have created a chronologically prioritized reading plan though the entire Bible that can be accessed at frc.org/Bible or simply by texting the word *Bible* to 67742.

— DAY 1 —

Today's Reading: Jeremiah 1

Verse of the Day

> "They will fight against you, but they shall not prevail against you. For I am with you," says the LORD, "to deliver you."
>
> *Jeremiah 1:19*

Please read the entire Scripture selection in your own Bible and highlight or underline verses that stand out to you before you read the observations and engage the questions below.

Let's begin in Jeremiah 1:1: "The words of Jeremiah the son of Hilkiah, of the priests who were in Anathoth in the land of Benjamin." Now quite a significant note here: Hilkiah, Jeremiah's father, was the high priest whom we read about over in 2 Kings 22; he found or rediscovered the book of the law in the temple after Manasseh had defiled it with idol worship. Now whether or not the priests of that day hid the word so that Manasseh wouldn't destroy it, Hilkiah discovered it during the time of Josiah's reform, cleansing of the temple, and reestablishing it. But when the Word was rediscovered, that's when the Lord brought the revival during Josiah's reign. Jeremiah 1:2–5:

> to whom the word of the LORD came in the days of Josiah the son of Amon, king of Judah, in the thirteenth year of his reign. It came also in the days of Jehoiakim the son of Josiah, king of Judah, until the end of the eleventh year of Zedekiah the

> son of Josiah, king of Judah, until the carrying away of Jerusalem captive in the fifth month. Then the word of the LORD came to me, saying: "Before I formed you in the womb I knew you; before you were born I sanctified you; I ordained you a prophet to the nations."

Now isn't it a good thing that Hilkiah the priest was not influenced by King Manasseh? Remember, Manasseh seduced the people to do all sorts of abominations, including sacrificing their children on the altar of Molech. Not unlike the sacrificing of children today on the altar of convenience, which we call abortion.

Let's continue in verse 6: "Then said I: 'Ah Lord GOD! Behold, I cannot speak, for I am a youth.'" Notice throughout Scripture where God uses individuals' humility that marks their lives by saying, "I'm incapable. I can't do this." Moses said the same thing. Well, it's not them; it's not us doing it ultimately. In Ephesians 6, Paul lays out how we're to live the Christian life, and he says, you're thinking, *How in the world are we going to do this?* We're to do it in the power and the might of the Lord. That's how. God works through us. It's not in our own strength or in our own ability. Yes, he's given us talents and we're to use those, but ultimately, we must rely upon God.

Look at the next few verses in Jeremiah 1, beginning with verse 7: "But the LORD said to me: 'Do not say, "I am a youth," for you shall go to all to whom I send you, and whatever I command you, you shall speak.'" Look at verses 8–10: "'Do not be afraid of their faces, for I am with you to deliver you,' says the LORD.' Then the LORD put forth His hand and touched my mouth, and the LORD said to me: 'Behold, I have put My words in your mouth. See, I have this day set you over the nations and over the kingdoms, to root out and to pull down, to destroy and to throw down, to build and to plant.'" God then goes on to use an almond branch and a boiling pot as illustrations to communicate a prophetic message in verses 11–14, something that we will see frequently throughout Jeremiah's ministry.

Now look at verses 15–16: "'For behold, I am calling all the families of the kingdoms of the north,' says the LORD; 'they shall come and each one set his throne at the entrance of the gates of Jerusalem, against all its walls all around, and against all the cities of Judah. I will utter My judgments against them concerning all their wickedness, because they have forsaken me, burned incense to other gods, and worshiped the works of their own hands." Obviously, there are many modern-day idols. People today worship the works of their own hands. So this has application to us. Verse 17: "'Therefore prepare yourself and arise, and speak to them all that I command you. Do not be dismayed before their faces, lest I dismay you before them.'" God was talking to Jeremiah about faithfully and fearlessly communicating every word he was given. God was saying, "Don't let them intimidate you, Jeremiah" because verse 18: "'For behold, I have made you this day a fortified city and an iron pillar, and bronze walls against the whole land—against the kings of Judah, against its princes, against its priests, and against the people of the land.'" Finally, here is why the "cancel crowd" of Jeremiah's day couldn't shut him down in verse 19: "'They will fight against you, but they shall not prevail against you. For I am with you,' says the LORD, 'to deliver you.'"

As followers of Jesus, we have that same promise. How? In Matthew 28, the Great Commission, Jesus tells His disciples and all of those who will follow Him through the generations, "Go therefore and make disciples of all nations, baptizing them in the name of the Father and of the Son and of the Holy Spirit, teaching them to observe all that I have commanded you" (vv. 19–20a). And listen to this: "And lo, I am with you always, even to the end of the age" (v. 20b). Now that doesn't mean we won't face opposition. That doesn't mean there won't be a cancel crowd, but it does mean we won't face it alone. And as we refuse to be afraid to speak the truth contained in the Word of God, what Jesus has taught us, God will prosper it. God will use it to accomplish the call that is upon our lives to reach others with the good news of Jesus Christ.

Questions for Reflection and Discussion

1. When did God call Jeremiah to be a prophet according to verse 1?
    a. When he was in the womb
    b. When he was a teenager
    c. When he was a senior adult
    d. None of the above

2. What was Jeremiah's assessment of his own capability in response to God's call (v. 6), and how did God respond to Jeremiah's reservations (v. 7)?

Notes on Today's Bible Reading

— DAY 2 —

Today's Reading: Jeremiah 2

Verse of the Day

> "For My people have committed two evils: They have forsaken Me, the fountain of living waters, and hewn themselves cisterns—broken cisterns that can hold no water."
>
> *Jeremiah 2:13*

Please read the entire Scripture selection in your own Bible and highlight or underline verses that stand out to you before you read the observations and engage the questions below.

What would lead a nation to trade the truth for a lie? Well, we're going to answer that question today as we look at Jeremiah 2. Now this was Jeremiah's first sermon, the first prophetic message after God commissioned him publicly as a prophet to the nations. Now he begins his ministry, and we looked at this timeline yesterday; he began his ministry in the thirteenth year of Josiah's reign. Now, that means Josiah was about twenty-one years old, almost the same age as Jeremiah. We think Jeremiah was approximately twenty when his ministry began.

As I mentioned yesterday, Jeremiah's father, Hilkiah was the priest that was involved in cleaning up the temple because it had been misused and neglected during the reign of Manasseh, Josiah's grandfather. And during that process, Hilkiah discovered the book of the law. This was God's Word, which the nation had been without. But this didn't happen until the eighteenth year of Josiah's reign, which was five years into the ministry of Jeremiah. This is important because these first six chapters roughly came before the rediscovery of God's Word. I'll give you some idea of Josiah's heart over in 2 Chronicles 34:3. It says that when Josiah was sixteen, "In the eighth year of his reign, while he was still young, he began to seek the God of his father David; and in the twelfth year he began to purge Judah and Jerusalem of the high places, the wooden images, the carved images, and the molded images." So a year before Jeremiah came onto the scene by God's calling, Josiah, in seeking God without authority, didn't have the Word; he just had a heart for God. But remember what God's Word says, "If you seek Me, you'll find Me." So he begins to seek God and begins to purge the city and Judah of the idolatry that had become rampant. And then God sent a prophet with a message that reinforced what the king was doing, that led to the rediscovery of the Word of God and a revival of sorts.

Let's start in Jeremiah 2:1: "Moreover the word of the Lord came to me, saying, 'Go and cry in the hearing of Jerusalem, saying, "Thus says the Lord: 'I remember you, the kindness of your youth, the love of your betrothal, when you went after Me in the wilderness, in a land not sown. Israel was holiness to the Lord, the firstfruits of His increase. All that devour him will offend; disaster will come upon them,' says the Lord."'" What's he saying there? Well, he's saying they left their first love. When they were in need, and they were struggling in the wilderness, they walked close to the Lord. But once they entered into the land of promise and experienced the blessings of God, they forgot God. This is not unlike what Jesus said over in Revelation 2 about the church of Ephesus. He said, "You have left your first love."

Let's jump down to verse 11: "Has a nation changed its gods, which are not gods?" He's actually saying, "Look at the heathen nations around you. Have they changed their gods?" "You've changed to gods that are not gods. But my people have changed their glory. The glory of God for what does not profit." Verses 12–13: "'Be astonished, O heavens, at this, and be horribly afraid; be very desolate,' says the Lord. 'For My people have committed two evils: They have forsaken Me, the fountain of living waters, and hewn themselves cisterns—broken cisterns that can hold no water.'" So here are the two evils: they forgot

God, then they embraced a knockoff over the real deal, trading living water for broken cisterns that would not hold water.

When I was a kid, we had a cistern. We didn't have city water until later. And I remember we had to ration water, especially in the summertime when it was hot, and we didn't get a lot of rain. But then when it would rain, you had to let the rain run for about five or ten minutes to clean off the roof of the house so all the debris would be washed away. Then you'd have to run outside and turn a valve on the downspouts to catch the water. And as the oldest, that was my job. No matter how hard it was raining or storming. Was I ever so glad when we got city water, when we didn't have to ration water, and I didn't have to run outside in storms to catch the water.

People in Jeremiah's time had the fountain of living water, and they traded for cisterns that won't hold water. It doesn't make sense. Look at the consequences, though, of this decision, of this choice in verse 19: "'Your own wickedness will correct you, and your backslidings will rebuke you. Know therefore and see that it is an evil and bitter thing that you have forsaken the LORD your God. And the fear of Me is not in you', says the Lord GOD of hosts." The consequences are evident, and they come from our own choices. He said, "Your wickedness will correct you." You're going to pay a price for your sin. This will come upon you. Your backslidings will reprove you.

When a nation trades the real relationship with God for idols, consequences come. Now how did this happen? What would lead a nation to trade the truth of God for a lie? Well, look at verses 7 and 8: "'I brought you into a bountiful country, to eat its fruit and its goodness. But when you entered, you defiled My land and made My heritage an abomination.'" How did they defile it? They defiled it with idolatry. "The priests did not say, 'Where is the LORD?' And those who handle the law did not know Me; the rulers also transgressed against Me; the prophets prophesied by Baal, and walked after things that do not profit." There was spiritual complacency because they didn't need God. They had everything they needed. Does that sound familiar? This was aided by a contempt for the truth; those who handled the law, they didn't know God. This is then fueled by political corruption—leaders who did not know God nor cared whether they offended God, which brings on moral and cultural chaos.

The people were spiritually complacent because they had become intoxicated with the blessings of God, so much so that they forgot God Himself. The keepers of the law, the elite of the day, then ran with their contempt for God and His truth. Civil leaders then paid no attention to God and abused their authority. And the preachers' final line of defense? The prophets and the preachers gave a popular word, a word people wanted to hear, not what they needed to hear. That is how a nation trades the truth for a lie.

What America needs right now are for preachers and Christian leaders to proclaim not their opinions, not their ideas, but the truth of God's Word. If you're in a church where the pastor or the preacher is more worried about offending the world by using the wrong pronoun than he is offending a holy God and leading His people astray, quite frankly it's time for a new church. Our greatest need in America is to rediscover the truth of God, and that is incumbent upon the ministers of God to proclaim that truth.

Questions for Reflection and Discussion

1. What caused God to bring charges against Israel in verses 5–9?
    a. Israel followed worthless idols.
    b. Priests did not seek the Lord.
    c. Rebellious religious leaders who dealt with the law did not know the Lord.
    d. Prophets prophesied by Baal.
    e. All of the above.

2. What two main sins did God say His people had committed according to verse 13?

Notes on Today's Bible Reading

— DAY 3 —

Today's Reading: Jeremiah 3

Verse of the Day

> "Return, backsliding Israel," says the Lord; "I will not cause My anger to fall on you. For I am merciful," says the Lord; "I will not remain angry forever."
>
> *Jeremiah 3:12*

Please read the entire Scripture selection in your own Bible and highlight or underline verses that stand out to you before you read the observations and engage the questions below.

The question is, When is it too late to turn to God? In this chapter, we see the word *backslide* or a variation of the Hebrew word *mishuvah* seven times. It appears eleven times in the Old Testament in total. Seven times out of the eleven it's in this chapter, nine times in Jeremiah, and two times in the book of Hosea. It means to turn away or turn back from God. Interestingly, we also see in this chapter the word *return* seven times. So, seven times we see the word *backslide* and seven times we see the word *return*.

Verses 1–5 are a continuation of Jeremiah's first sermon after his public commissioning that we read in chapter 2. We're going to move to a second sermon, but I want to draw your attention to a couple of things first. Look at verses 2–3a: "'Lift up your eyes to the desolate heights and see: Where have you not lain with men? By the road you have set for them like an Arabian in the wilderness; and you have polluted the land with your harlotries and your wickedness. Therefore the showers have been withheld, and there has been no latter rain.'" The idolatry that was in these high places, where there were groves of trees, not only involved the worship of idols (or in reality demonic beings; see Deut. 32:16–17), but it was also the site of sexual immorality and drunkenness.

You have to ask the question, Why is idolatry popular? Well, looking at it from a dispassionate perspective, it looks foolish. It really does. Picture an otherwise rational human being bowing down to a piece of carved wood or stone. But the reason idolatry is popular is it affirms and even demands that people engage, without boundaries, the desire of human nature. By contrast, the call of Christ is to deny ourselves, die to this world and those things of this world (see Luke 9:23), and seek those things that are above (see Col. 3:1). So what's the difference? Idolatry says, "Hey, do whatever you want. If it feels good, do it"; whereas the call of Christ is to deny ourselves and our earthly desires and seek those things that are above. But I want to draw your attention to this next thing. What does verse 3 say? Was the crisis in the climate or the environment they were experiencing the result of the spiritual climate? After he says what they had been doing, he went on: "Therefore the showers have been withheld, and there has been no latter rain." Was this climate crisis the result of turning away from God? That's what the Bible says.

Let's go on to the second sermon, which he begins preaching in verse 6. Here God pointed to the kingdom of Israel and told Jeremiah to preach, to proclaim to the ten northern tribes. Remember, Jeremiah was a prophet to the two southern tribes of Judah. And God told him to turn to the north and speak to them as an example of what happens when you turn away from God and you continue in idolatry and immorality. As result, they were defeated then carried away as captives into Assyria. Look at what he says in verse 7: "'And I said, after she [Israel] had done all these things, "Return to Me." But she did not return. And her treacherous sister Judah saw it.'" Now jump to verse 10: "'And yet for all this her treacherous sister Judah has not turned to Me with her whole heart, but in pretense,' says the Lord." He was saying, "Look, they were carried away because of their sin and idolatry. You saw this, but yet you did not turn to me except in pretense." So there was a revival, but as we'll see throughout the book of Jeremiah, it was quite superficial. It was not the transformational experience it could have been, saving them from the coming Babylonian captivity.

Let's go now to verses 12–15, where he's still speaking to the southern tribes but doing so by speaking to the northern tribes.

> "Go and proclaim these words toward the north, and say: 'Return, backsliding Israel,' says the LORD; 'I will not cause My anger to fall on you. For I am merciful,' says the LORD; 'I will not remain angry forever. Only acknowledge your iniquity, that you have transgressed against the LORD your God, and have scattered your charms to alien deities under every green tree, and you have not obeyed My voice,' says the LORD. Return, O backsliding children," says the LORD; "for I am married to you. I will take you, one from a city and two from a family, and I will bring you to Zion. And I will give you shepherds according to My heart, who will feed you with knowledge and understanding."

Now jump over to verse 22: "'Return, you backsliding children, and I will heal your backslidings.' Indeed we do come to You, for You are the LORD our God." This is the answer to our question, When is it too late to return to God? Never. As long as you are breathing and on this side of eternity, it is not too late to return to God. First John 1:9 says, "If we confess our sins, He is faithful and just to forgive us our sins and cleanse us from all unrighteousness." There's no limit to the mercy of God. Here He was saying to the children of Israel, "Look, you've already been carried into captivity. You've sinned, you've rejected me, you've turned away, you've backslidden. But I'm merciful. If you will turn to me and confess your iniquities"—look what He says He'll do—"I will restore." God told Jeremiah to proclaim this to Assyria where the northern tribes had been carried away. He says, "Return to me and I will forgive your sin, I will restore you to the land, and I'll provide for you. I'll provide shepherds according to my heart." In other words, leaders who would guide them in the right way. It's never too late for people to turn back to God.

Questions for Reflection and Discussion

1. To what did God compare Judah to illustrate their sin of idolatry (see vv. 1–10)?
   a. A disobedient child
   b. A rebellious teen
   c. An adulterous wife
   d. A stubborn man
   e. None of the above

2. What promises did God make to faithless Israel if only she would return to Him and acknowledge her guilt (see vv. 11–18)?
   a. I will not be angry forever.
   b. I will bring you to Zion.
   c. I will give you shepherds (leaders) after my own heart.
   d. The house of Judah will follow the house of Israel and come back to the land of their inheritance.
   e. All of the above.

Notes on Today's Bible Reading

— DAY 4 —

Today's Reading: Jeremiah 4

Verse of the Day

> For thus says the Lord to the men of Judah and Jerusalem: "Break up your fallow ground, and do not sow among thorns."
>
> *Jeremiah 4:3*

Please read the entire Scripture selection in your own Bible and highlight or underline verses that stand out to you before you read the observations and engage the questions below.

What does hard ground have to do with our hearts? Well in Jeremiah 4, God compares the hearts of his people to "fallow ground," a farmer's field that has been unattended for some time (v. 3). At the very least, it needs to be broken up, plowed, and tilled. It may even need to be burned because leaving land untended for a few seasons allows it to become overgrown with noxious weeds and thorns. Without preparation, sowing it with good seed would be useless. Even if some of the seed penetrated that hard-packed ground, the crops would get choked out by the thorns. Jesus spoke of this problem in His parable of the sower (Matt. 13:18–23), explaining God's Word that falls onto a hard heart or onto a weed-choked heart ultimately produces little or nothing. Satan comes and snatches away some, and the competing culture chokes out others. Spiritual fruit cannot grow and thrive in such soil. The remedy is to break up the fallow ground of the heart, which involves our humble repentance.

Then Jeremiah shifts in verse 4 to another comparison that his audience could relate to: "'Circumcise yourselves to the LORD, and take away the foreskins of your hearts, you men of Judah and inhabitants of Jerusalem, lest my fury come forth like fire, and burn so that no one can quench it, because of the evil of your doings." Comparing ritual circumcision to the need for spiritual circumcision of the heart was not original with Jeremiah. Moses spoke of this need back in Deuteronomy (see 10:16; 30:6). Again, the remedy is humble repentance, which would prevent God's impending judgment.

In fact, two declarations of God's coming judgment are in verses 5–13. In verses 5–10, God instructed Jeremiah to blow the trumpet and raise the standard as a warning that an invasion was coming from the north (vv. 5–6). The invader is like a lion who will lay waste to the land (v. 7). The needed response? Verse 8: "For this, clothe yourself with sackcloth, lament and wail. For the fierce anger of the LORD has not turned back from us." The second declaration in verses 11–13 speaks of God's judgment being unleashed like a powerful wind. It will be swift: "'Behold, he shall come up like clouds, and his chariots like a whirlwind. His horses are swifter than eagles. Woe to us, for we are plundered!" (v. 13). The needed response? Look at verse 14: "O Jerusalem, wash your heart from wickedness, that you may be saved. How long shall your evil thoughts lodge within you?" In fact, verses 14–18 are a call to look within.

In verses 19–21, Jeremiah prophetically assumed the anguish of a person whose land has been plundered by an invading army. However, in verse 22, God Himself spoke to the sad condition of His people: "'For My people are foolish, they have not known Me. They are silly children, and they have no understanding. They are wise to do evil, but to do good they have no knowledge.'" Though the Lord would send harsh judgment via a devastating invasion, it would not be final. Look at verse 27: "'The whole land shall be desolate; yet I will not make a full end." Even in judgment, God will remember mercy (see Hab. 3:2). Yet we should not presume on His mercy. We don't have to follow Judah into judgment. We should deal with our sin before God's disciplinary judgment comes with swift and painful consequences. Paul, in his letter to the believers at Corinth said, "For if we would judge ourselves, we would not be judged (1 Cor. 11:31). God is graciously and patiently waiting. Let's not disappoint Him with our delay but run to Him with our repentance.

Questions for Reflection and Discussion

1. In verse 1, what was God's prescription for God's sinful people?
    a. Return to the Lord
    b. Remove their idols
    c. Renew their allegiance to the Lord
    d. All of the above

2. In the day of Judah's judgment, what are the responses of her king, her priests, and her prophets (v. 9)?

Notes on Today's Bible Reading

— DAY 5 —

Today's Reading: Jeremiah 5

Verse of the Day

> "An astonishing and horrible thing has been committed in the land."
>
> *Jeremiah 5:30*

Please read the entire Scripture selection in your own Bible and highlight or underline verses that stand out to you before you read the observations and engage the questions below.

An astonishing and horrible thing" was committed in the land. What was this astonishing and horrible thing? The last verse of chapter 5 tells us. But before we look at that, we need to look at the consequences of this horrible thing. So we're going to begin in Jeremiah 5:1–2: "Run to and fro through the streets of Jerusalem; see now and know; and seek in her open places if you can find a man, if there is anyone who executes judgment, who seeks the truth, and I will pardon her. Though they say, 'As the LORD lives,' Surely, they swear falsely." Sounds like Sodom and Gomorrah when Abraham was negotiating with God, saying, "If I can find just 100 righteous all the way down to ten, will you spare the city?" So truth had departed. That was one of the consequences of this horrible thing. Truth had departed.

Now jump down to verse 7a: "'How shall I pardon you for this? Your children have forsaken Me and sworn by those that are not gods.'" God was forgotten. This was another one of the consequences of this horrible thing. Look at verses 8–9a: "'They were like well-fed lusty stallions; every one neighed after his neighbor's wife. Shall I not punish them for these things?' says the Lord." He used this illustration of horses neighing after another horse. Sex was a preoccupation. We see that throughout these first six chapters because adultery or sexual fornication was a part of the idolatry in many cases.

Look at verses 12–13: "They have lied about the Lord, and said, 'It is not He. Neither will evil come upon us, nor shall we see sword or famine. And the prophets become wind, for the word is not in them. Thus shall it be done to them.'" Reality was denied. We see this later where the prophets were saying, "Peace, peace." Or basically, "There's no trouble. Everything's fine." But it wasn't. So reality was denied. Now look at how God responded to this in verse 22: "'Do you not fear me?' says the Lord. 'Will you not tremble at My presence, who have placed the sand as the bound of the sea, by a perpetual decree, that it cannot pass beyond it? And though its waves toss to and fro, yet they cannot prevail; though they roar, yet they cannot pass over it.'" He's saying, "You don't fear Me, the Creator, the one who set the boundaries of creation. You have no fear of Me." So fear of God had been lost. The astonishing and horrible thing was the cause of this moral and spiritual meltdown of the nation that put them in the HOV lane for God's judgment.

Let's look at what this horrible and astonishing thing was. Look at verses 30–31: "'An astonishing and horrible thing has been committed in the land: The prophets prophesy falsely, and the priests rule by their own power; and My people love to have it so. But what will you do in the end?'" The prophets prophesied falsely. Jeremiah spoke to these prophets. This is mentioned in Jeremiah 6:14, which says, "'They have also healed the hurt of My people slightly, saying, "Peace, peace!" When there is no peace.'" In other words, "Don't worry, the best is yet to come, we're fine. Don't worry about these minor setbacks. They're not from God. This is global warming. Not God's warning about our sin." But there's more. Look over at Jeremiah 23:14: "'Also I have seen a horrible thing in the prophets of Jerusalem: They commit adultery and walk in lies; they also strengthen the hands of the evildoers, so that no one turns back from his wickedness. All of them are like Sodom to Me, and her inhabitants like Gomorrah."

My understanding of the prophets in the church age after the canon of Scripture was closed is primarily not giving a new word about what was going to occur but, rather, proclaiming the written Word of God and application to our world today—a prophetic voice. The church is to have a prophetic voice today. One of my favorite quotes from Dr. Martin Luther King Jr. is, "The church must be reminded that it is not the master or the servant of the state, but rather the conscience of the state. It must be the guide and the critic of the state and never its tool. If the church does not recapture its prophetic zeal, it will become an irrelevant social club without moral or spiritual authority." Paul spoke to this in his final letter to Timothy before he is executed in Rome. Second Timothy 4:1–5 says,

> I charge you therefore before God and the Lord Jesus Christ, who will judge the living and the dead at His appearing and His kingdom: Preach the word! Be ready in season and out of season. Convince, rebuke, exhort, with all longsuffering and teaching. For the time will come when they will not endure sound doctrine, but according to their own desires, because they have itching ears, they will heap up for themselves teachers; and they will turn their ears away from the truth, and be turned aside to fables. But you be watchful in all things, endure afflictions, do the work of an evangelist, fulfill your ministry.

Now we see secondly that the priests ruled by their own power. And in that day, there was not a separation of church and state as we have today. Now we want separation. We do. That's the way God designed it. When you hear separation of church and state today, though, from the Left, what they're really saying is separation of God and government, meaning God and His Word must be kept out of government. That is not the case. While they are free to bring their humanist ideals and philosophies into government, Christians are expected to check their faith at the door of government. And we can never, ever agree to such terms.

Under the system of government in the Old Testament, the priests were the judges. The prophets were more like today's preachers, and the priests were the judges dispensing justice to the people. Here we read that they did it by their own power. What does that mean? They had departed from transcendent truth. They had departed from the truth of God, the moral law of God, the moral absolutes that govern the universe. In other words, moral relativism, which is what we see today in this postmodern world in which we live.

Now third, the people love to have it so. Why? Because they were not challenged by or held account to the truth of God. So here's a hard truth (and I've seen this up close and personal in my time in government, even as an elected official): In a nation like ours, the leaders we have reflect who we are as a nation, as a whole. The people love to have it so. Many of us don't want leaders that will challenge us to walk with God or set an example, a strong moral and spiritual example. This is especially true in a republic like ours where we have the freedom and the ability to elect our own leaders. And this predates the controversy of the November 2020 election.

As we finish, keep in mind that God's warnings through His prophets, Jeremiah and others, were all about one objective: seeing people return to Him. You see, God doesn't need to warn us that judgment is coming again; He can just do it. But His purpose in sending this message is to bring about conviction of our sins so that we might repent and experience the mercy of God. Let's pray that America, beginning in the church, will return to God. And if the church returns to God, I believe it will have a tremendous effect. And when I say return, I mean that we seek first the kingdom of God and His righteousness and all these other things will be added. That we live out our faith in such a way that it impacts and challenges and transforms the world around us in America, and we'll have the benefit of experiencing the blessings of God again.

Questions for Reflection and Discussion

1. What kind of person was to be searched for according to verse 1?
    a. Seeks justice
    b. Seeks truth
    c. Both of the above
    d. Neither of the above

2. What "astonishing and horrible thing" had occurred in the land according to verse 31?

Notes on Today's Bible Reading

— DAY 6 —

Today's Reading: Jeremiah 6

Verse of the Day

> Thus says the LORD: "Stand in the ways and see, and ask for the old paths, where the good way is, and walk in it; then you will find rest for your souls. But they said, 'We will not walk in it.'"
>
> *Jeremiah 6:16*

Please read the entire Scripture selection in your own Bible and highlight or underline verses that stand out to you before you read the observations and engage the questions below.

Is there a first step on the road to judgment? That's what we're going to look at today. This is important. Have you've ever been lost in the woods, and you've tried to find your way out? You retrace your steps, and you can go back to where you made a wrong turn or where you went the wrong direction. Let's see if this passage has some insight into the question, Where does a nation go wrong?

Chapter 6 of Jeremiah is the last of Jeremiah's messages warning the southern tribe of Judah during the reign of Josiah. The focus in this chapter is similar to what it is in the previous chapters. Judgment was coming. The Babylonians would be invading. They would lay siege to Jerusalem. And the reason was the pervasive sin of the nation. So let's start near the end of the chapter, which speaks to the fact the nation had become evil to the core. The Lord spoke to Jeremiah in 6:27–30: "'I have set you as an assayer and a fortress among My people, that you may know and test their way. They are all stubborn rebels, walking as slanderers. They are bronze and iron, they are all corrupters; the bellows blow fiercely, the lead is consumed by the fire; the smelter refines in vain, for the wicked are not drawn off. People will call them rejected silver, because the LORD has rejected them.'" So what is He saying here? There are a lot of illustrations—of course in terminology they would understand in that day. We may not be as familiar with this; when silver is put into a refining fire, the dross, the alloys, is removed so that the silver has value. God said the refining fire that's been applied to them was discovering the alloy was so thick within the silver, it is so full of the alloy, there's no separating it. They were worthless. It was a worthless silver.

We see a description here of what they had become as a nation in Jeremiah 6:6–7: "For thus has the LORD of hosts said: 'Cut down trees, and build a mound against Jerusalem. This is the city to be punished. She is full of oppression in her midst. As a fountain wells up with water, so she wells up with her wickedness. Violence and plundering are heard in her. Before Me continually are grief and wounds." So they had become a nation of violence and oppression. They were a worldly nation. They were a consumer nation. Look at verse 13a: "'Because from the least of them even to the greatest of them, everyone is given to covetousness.'" It was all about more. They were ungrateful. And that's part of it. We humans always want something else, want something someone else has. Envious, not satisfied and grateful for what we've been given. The prophets who said what the people wanted to hear, not what they needed to hear, were just corrupt. Look at what it says in the second half of verse 13 then 14: "'And from the prophet even to the priest, everyone deals falsely. They have also healed the hurt of My people slightly, saying, "Peace, peace!" When there is no peace.'" Instead of dealing with the underlying issues that were leading to judgment, they said, "Oh, it's OK. Peace, peace." But there was no peace. There was no shame in their sin. In fact, they celebrated their sin and took pride in it. Look at verse 15a: "'Were they ashamed when they had committed abomination?'" What kind of abominations? Remember, idolatry, sexual immorality. And on top of this, they put on a religious show but rejected the lordship of God. Look over in verses 17–18: "'Also, I set watchmen over you, saying, "Listen to the sound of the trumpet!" But they said, "We will not listen." Therefore hear, you nations, and know, O congregation, what is among them.'" But how did this happen? How did they become a city of violence and oppression, a worldly consumer nation, prophets who spoke what the people wanted to hear, not what God had instructed them to say? There was no shame in their sin; they celebrated it! They had a religious air about them but no relationship with their Creator. How did it happen? Well, I believe this passage shows us that first step on the road to rejection and to judgment.

Look at verses 10–11: "To whom shall I speak and give warning, that they may hear? Indeed their ear is uncircumcised, and they cannot give heed. Behold, the word of the LORD is a reproach to them; they have no delight in it. Therefore I am full of the fury of the LORD. I am weary of holding it in. 'I will pour it out on the children outside, and on the assembly of young men together; for even the husband shall be taken with the wife, the aged with him who is full of days.'"

Judgment was coming. They rejected the Word of Lord. They would not hear the Word of Lord. In fact, it had become an object of scorn. They mocked the Word of God. Look at verse 16: "Thus says the LORD: 'Stand in the ways and see, and ask for the old paths, where the good way is, and walk in it; then you will find rest for your souls.'" God gave them the answer: "Go back to the truth. Walk in those ways and you will find rest for your souls." But verse 16 goes on to say, "But they said, 'We will not walk in it.'" You see, they had rejected the Word of the Lord. They refused to listen and yield to the Word of Lord. They closed their ears to what God was saying. That is the first step on this path of pervasive sin that leads to the judgment of God. You know, we must return to the Word of God and not be only hearers of the word, but doers of the word as well.

As James 1:22 says, "But be doers of the word, and not hearers only, deceiving yourselves." We need to be doing the Word of the Lord as we hear it, beginning in our homes. It needs to define our churches. Our churches must be places where the Word is preached. If you're in a church that, you know, you hear these nice topical sermons that really do not go into the Word of God, you need to find another church. Our churches need to be marked by the Word of God, defined by the Word of God, and so does our nation. A defining characteristic of our nation once again needs to be the Word of God.

Questions for Reflection and Discussion

1. What were most prophets and priests guilty of according to verse 14?

2. What was the Lord pleading with the people to do in verse 16?
    a. Ask for the ancient paths
    b. Walk in the good way
    c. Find rest for your souls
    d. All of the above

Notes on Today's Bible Reading

— DAY 7 —

Today's Reading: Jeremiah 7

Verse of the Day

> "Do not trust in these lying words, saying, 'The temple of the LORD, the temple of the LORD, the temple of the LORD are these.'"
>
> *Jeremiah 7:4*

Please read the entire Scripture selection in your own Bible and highlight or underline verses that stand out to you before you read the observations and engage the questions below.

Don't go to church. Why? Stick with me. I'll explain. We're moving into a new area of Jeremiah's ministry. In chapter 1, we had his calling and commission. Chapters 2–6 took place during the time of Josiah, a good king who brought about spiritual reform. But as we will see, it was without spiritual revival, which did not lead to the reformation of the people. The next thirteen chapters reflect the reigns of Jehoiakim and Josiah. Now, to give you further context, Josiah had torn down the high places, the temple had been cleaned up, and it had been restored. And in that process, Hilkiah, Jeremiah's father, had discovered the Torah, the law of Moses, which either had been forgotten or had been hidden. Maybe the priest had hidden it, thinking that a prior king, Manasseh, would destroy it. But whatever the case was, they found it. The temple was now open again, and people began to gather in the temple.

Jeremiah mostly likely brought the message in chapter 7 at the entrance of the gates during one of the three major Jewish feasts called for in the Torah, but we will see that something was missing among the people. Look at verses 1–4: "The word that came to Jeremiah from the LORD, saying, 'Stand in the gate of the LORD's house, and proclaim there this word, and say, "Hear the word of the LORD, all you of Judah who enter in at these gates to worship the LORD!"' Thus says the LORD of hosts, the God of Israel: 'Amend your ways and your doings, and I will cause you to dwell in this place. Do not trust in these lying words, saying, "The temple of the LORD, the temple of the LORD, the temple of the LORD are these."'"

What does that mean? Well, during the reign of Hezekiah, about one hundred years previously, God miraculously delivered Jerusalem from the king of Assyria, Sennacherib. They were surrounded. They were under siege. Yet in 2 Kings 19 (see also Isa. 37), they were miraculously delivered. However, the people were convinced it was the temple in their presence, not the presence of God in His power that had delivered them. So now that the temple had been restored, the people were persuaded that Jeremiah's preaching and his messages of warning were simply negative vibes from a radical preacher. They wanted to hear positive, encouraging words, even though they were false words.

Let's continue in Jeremiah 7:5–7: "'For if you thoroughly amend your ways and your doings, if you thoroughly execute judgment between a man and his neighbor, if you do not oppress the stranger, the fatherless, and the widow, and do not shed innocent blood in this place, or walk after other gods to your hurt, then I will cause you to dwell in this place, in the land that I gave to your fathers forever and ever.'" What is he saying? He's saying, "Repent, repent," which means to turn. Turn from your sin, and you'll be in good shape if you will repent and turn from your sin. Guess what? Yes, you'll be able to stay in this land. It won't be the temple that delivers you. It'll be My presence and My power.

Look over at verses 8–10: "'Behold, you trust in lying words that cannot profit. Will you steal, murder, commit adultery, swear falsely, burn incense to Baal, and walk after other gods whom you do not know, and then come and stand before Me in this house which is called by My name, and say, "We are delivered to do all these abominations"?'" This is what Dietrich Bonhoeffer wrote about in his book *The Cost of Discipleship* when he talked about cheap grace. Listen to this quote: "Cheap grace is the preaching of forgiveness without requiring repentance, baptism without church discipline, communion without confession, absolution without personal confession. Cheap grace is grace without discipleship, grace without the cross, grace without Jesus Christ living and incarnate."[1]

You see, they were just going to church, but God doesn't want us just to go to church, thinking we can live how we want. They hadn't changed their ways, they were still involved in the idols, and they were still involved in sexual immorality. They were still oppressing people. They had not changed their ways. But they said, "Oh, we've got the temple. God is here again. That's cheap grace. What distinguishes us in the eyes of God is not our religious ritual; it's our relationship with Him. But you ask, "What does that relationship look like?" It is trusting Jesus Christ as our Lord and Savior and receiving forgiveness of our sins. Then he talks about obeying God. Does that not apply to us today? Look at what Jesus says in John 14:15: "If you love Me, keep my commandments." You see, we don't keep God's commandments to get His love and express our love. We Love Him; therefore, we obey Him. Because when our hearts are changed through that transformative relationship with Jesus Christ, we want to obey Him.

Look at Jeremiah 7:11–12: "'Has this house, which is called by My name, become a den of thieves in your eyes? Behold, I, even I, have seen it,' says the LORD. 'But go now to My place which was in Shiloh, where I set My name at the first, and see what I did to it because of the wickedness of My people Israel.'" I've been to Shiloh many times, and it's in the eastern portion of Israel in the area the Bible calls Judea and Samaria. Now, of course, the politically correct term is West Bank, which I refuse to use. Shiloh is one of my favorite places to go in Israel because it is a reminder of the consequences of our choices. For

369 years, the presence of God was in this place in Shiloh. In fact, you go there today, you can see the outline of where the tabernacle was. The stones that were the foundation of the base for it are still there. And you look around, and literally there are hundreds of thousands of pottery shards from the offerings made, the vessels that were broken. But it all ended in one day because of spiritual and moral compromise. It took years to get to that point, but for 369 years the presence of God was there. Think about that. That's almost as long as America has been in existence, from the time the Jamestown settlers came to Virginia and the Pilgrims landed at Plymouth. For almost 400 years, it had been the center of Jewish life, and it all ended in a day because of spiritual and moral compromise.

Let's go to verses 13–14: "'And now, because you have done all these works,' says the LORD, 'and I spoke to you, rising up early and speaking, but you did not hear, and I called you, but you did not answer, therefore I will do to the house which is called by My name, in which you trust, and to this place which I gave to you and your fathers, as I have done to Shiloh.'" In other words, He said, "You're trusting in this building. This building is not going to save you." Going to church is not going to save you. The fact that America goes to church is not going to matter. Is it important? Absolutely. But more important is what is happening in our hearts because as believers *we are* the temple of God (see 1 Cor. 3:16–17; 6:19–20; Eph. 2:19–22; 1 Pet. 2:5).

So what's needed? Repentance. For what? You can see it here in Jeremiah 7. Verse 20 talks about the need for repentance for rejecting God's truth, and verses 30–32 talk about their idolatry and child sacrifice. And the bottom line can be summarized by 2 Chronicles 7:14, which says, "If My people who are called by My name will humble themselves, and pray and seek My face, and turn from their wicked ways, then I will hear from heaven, and will forgive their sin and heal their land." Don't go to church thinking that will save you or protect you. Allow God, by His grace, to change your heart and then obey Him. That is the best security this nation could ever have.

Questions for Reflection and Discussion

1. How many of the Ten Commandments had the people broken according to verses 9–10?

2. Why did God tell Jeremiah not to pray for His disobedient people according to verses 16–19?

Notes on Today's Bible Reading

— DAY 8 —

Today's Reading: Jeremiah 8

Verse of the Day

> "Behold, they have rejected the word of the Lord; so what wisdom do they have?"
>
> *Jeremiah 8:9b*

Please read the entire Scripture selection in your own Bible and highlight or underline verses that stand out to you before you read the observations and engage the questions below.

Is America an enlightened nation? Are we a wise nation? Well, we're going to take a look at that. The first three verses of chapter 8 are really a continuation of the message we see in Jeremiah 7. He talked about a backslidden people refusing to return to God, and, therefore, judgment was coming. Yet they continued in their ways, refusing to listen. Look at Jeremiah 8:10–12:

> "Therefore I will give their wives to others, and their fields to those who will inherit them; because from the least even to the greatest everyone is given to covetousness; from the prophet even to the priest everyone deals falsely. For they have healed the hurt of the daughter of My people slightly, saying, 'Peace, peace!' when there is no peace. Were they ashamed when they had committed abomination? No! They were not at all ashamed, nor did they know how to blush. Therefore they

> shall fall among those who fall; in the time of their punishment they shall be cast down," says the LORD.

We read that before.

This is really the same list we saw in 6:14: "'They have also healed the hurt of My people slightly, saying, "Peace, peace!" when there is no peace.'" He talked about the prophets there who were saying, "Oh, everything's going to be fine. It's positive, it's encouraging, everything's good. Nothing's happening." But in fact, judgment was coming because they had rejected the Word of God. You see, the role of the prophet is to speak truth. That doesn't mean it's going to be pleasant. It doesn't mean everyone's going to receive it. As I said, the role of the church in the world today is to be a prophetic voice, not to blend in, not to just be a different version of the world. We are to stand in sharp contrast, proclaiming truth. And the darker the culture becomes, the brighter the light of the church should be. In the prophetic word, it is proclaiming the written Word of God, the truth of God in its application to the world in which we live. Look at verse 15: "'Were they ashamed when they had committed abomination? No! They were not at all ashamed, nor did they know how to blush.'"

As I said, this is almost identical to chapter 6. Their hearts were so corrupted they took pride in their sin. What was their sin again? Well, we saw that they coveted what their neighbors had. They were consumers. They were never satisfied. And we also saw idolatry. Of course, as we've talked about before, in that idolatry and this pagan worship, there was sexual immorality. There was just total breakdown of the morals of society. So not only did they not blush; they celebrated it. And since the fall of man, sin has been in the world, and it will remain in the world until the ultimate reign of Christ. But sin is constrained by the moral standards of a society. And where do those standards come from? Well, they are provided in the Word of God, although as Paul writes in Romans 2, the moral law of God is written on our hearts just as God created the physical laws that govern the universe. So, there are moral laws that apply to all of us. They apply to all people at all times and all places. For instance, in every culture, it's wrong to murder. But how do they come up with it? Did they have a world meeting to decide that? No, it's written on the hearts of humankind. But you can reject this truth by suppressing it, which can be done in a multitude of ways.

Jeremiah here lays out again in 8:8–9 the root cause of their sin: "'How can you say, "We are wise, and the law of the LORD is with us"? Look, the false pen of the scribe certainly works falsehood. The wise men are ashamed, they are dismayed and taken. Behold, they have rejected the word of the LORD; so what wisdom do they have?'" Now, I know I'm starting to sound like a broken record, but Jeremiah once again points back to the cause of their sin. It is a rejection of the Word of God, pure and simple. They thought they were wise, but they had replaced God's Word with their own words of wisdom.

Now you see where I'm going with this. Think about all the focus placed on education today; you rarely hear a political leader speak without bringing up education. The key is more educational opportunities. Want a better future? We need more educational opportunities, more early childhood education. We're talking about two- and three-year-olds going to school. Expand access to postsecondary education. I mean, we have some calling for total government funding of college tuition. But this is not new. Education has been the focal point of political leaders for decades, if not going on centuries.

Still, think about this for a moment. With all of the focus on public education and all the tax dollars that flow to it—federal, state, and local—why did the scores on our national assessment tests continue to decline? Now, I can point to a dozen different answers, but there is one that is at the heart of the issue and we read it in verse 9: "Behold, they have rejected the word of the LORD; so what wisdom do they have?" God's people were special; they were exceptional because they had His Word. It was the secret to successful living. He laid out the roadmap for them, saying, Look, I'm going to give you this. You follow this, and you're going to be a blessed nation. He gave them the key to success.

Today, the church has the Word of God, and I know the broader culture is indifferent, if not hostile, to the Word of God. But that doesn't matter as Christians. We, as followers of Jesus Christ, must return, embrace, and live out the Word of God, even more so as there is hostility toward it. It's insufficient only to hear the Word. We must apply it and live it out, as James 1:22 says, "Be doers of the word, and not hearers only, deceiving yourselves."

Questions for Reflection and Discussion

1. With what does Jeremiah contrast the people's disobedience of God's judgments, rules, and decrees (see v. 7)?

2. What were some of the ways prophets and priests alike practiced deceit (see v. 10)?
   a. They treated the spiritual wounds of the people as if not serious.
   b. They cried, "Peace, Peace" when there was no peace.
   c. They had no shame and did not even know how to blush.
   d. All of the above.

Notes on Today's Bible Reading

— DAY 9 —

Today's Reading: Jeremiah 9

Verse of the Day

> "But let him who glories glory in this, that he understands and knows Me, that I am the LORD, exercising lovingkindness, judgment, and righteousness in the earth. For in these I delight," says the LORD.
>
> *Jeremiah 9:24*

Please read the entire Scripture selection in your own Bible and highlight or underline verses that stand out to you before you read the observations and engage the questions below.

What does God delight in? Well, stick around because that's the question we are going to answer. In this chapter, the prophet continues his warning to the people of God regarding His pending judgment. But here we see three things: the heart of the prophet, the heart of the people, and the heart of God.

First, let's look at the heart of the prophet. We see this in verses 1–3: "Oh, that my head were waters, and my eyes a fountain of tears, that I might weep day and night for the slain of the daughter of my people! Oh, that I had in the wilderness a lodging place for travelers; that I might leave my people, and go from them! For they are all adulterers, an assembly of treacherous men. 'And like their bow they have bent their tongues for lies. They are not valiant for the truth on the earth. For they proceed from evil to evil, and they do not know Me,' says the LORD."

The heart of the prophet was broken over the sin of the people and of the coming judgment of God. He saw clearly as a prophet. He connected the dots. He saw what was coming. God told him. But this is the nature of God. He is the same yesterday, today, and forever. And Jeremiah saw this, and so his heart was broken.

You recall Jeremiah was not eager for this assignment or this job as a prophet. He did not relish in proclaiming the coming judgment of God upon his people. He was grieved both by their sin and what he knew this was leading to. Now remember when Jesus asked His disciples, in Matthew 16:13b–14, "'Who do men say that I, the Son of Man, am?' So they said, 'Some say John the Baptist, some Elijah, and others Jeremiah or one of the prophets.'" Why Jeremiah? Well, I mentioned earlier in our reading of Jeremiah, he was the weeping prophet. Remember what Jesus said in Matthew 23:37: "'O Jerusalem, Jerusalem, the one who kills the prophets and stones those who were sent to her! How often I wanted to gather your children together, as a hen gathers her chicks under her wings, but you were not willing!'" Jesus was standing there looking at Jerusalem. His heart was broken for His people.

You know, our hearts need to be broken for what breaks the heart of God. What breaks His heart is our sin, the separation that exists between God and those He created to have fellowship with Him. That is why He sent Jesus. Look at John 3:16, a verse that most of us know: "For God so loved the world that He gave His only begotten Son, that whoever believes in Him should not perish but have everlasting life." See, Jeremiah did not speak the truth of God in a condescending or arrogant way, but he spoke the truth in love as Ephesians 4:15 says. He spoke the truth out of a redemptive heart. His heart was to see people come to the truth he was speaking, so they might be free from the bondage of sin. And the same should apply to us today. The reason we speak truths over the issues of our day—whether it's human sexuality, whether it's the sanctity of human life, and so on—is the fact we are created by God; we're not an accident. We speak that truth not to win a debate. Yes, we need to know the truth, and we need to have the facts. But we need to speak the truth so others might come to know the Truth, Jesus Christ. He said, "'I am the way, the truth, and the life. No one comes to the Father except through Me" (John 14:6). And He said, the truth will make you free (John 8:32). And so we speak the truth so others might be free.

Now let's look quickly at the heart of the people. We see this in Jeremiah 9:3–6: "'They are not valiant for the truth on the earth. For they proceed from evil to evil, and they do not know Me,' says the LORD. 'Everyone take heed to his neighbor, and do not trust any brother; for every brother will utterly supplant, and every neighbor will walk with slanderers. Everyone will deceive his neighbor, and will not speak the truth; they have taught their tongue to speak lies; they weary themselves to commit iniquity. Your dwelling place is in the midst of deceit; through deceit they refuse to know Me,' says the LORD."

They were not valiant for the truth. That is an understatement. They were not defenders of the truth. Rather, they were driven by evil. They didn't know the Lord, and as a result, they were deceitful with their neighbors. Why was this the case? Well, look at verses 13–14: "'Because they have forsaken My law which I set before them, and have not obeyed My voice, nor walked according to it, but they have walked according to the dictates of their own hearts and after the Baals, which their fathers taught them." So they couldn't walk in the truth. The currency they dealt in was false, so they couldn't be truthful with one another. Now recall when Jesus was asked what the greatest commandment is in Matthew 22:37–40. He said, "'You shall love the LORD your God with all your heart, with all your soul, and with all your mind.' This is the first and great commandment. And the second is like it: 'You shall love your neighbor as yourself.' On these two commandments hang all the Law and the Prophets.'" See, our relationship with God shapes and directs our relationships with others. When a people have forsaken God, the truth, they will not be truthful with one another. We cannot operate in the currency of truth when we work with and deal with a counterfeit message, a counterfeit worldview.

Now let's look at the heart of God. Look at Jeremiah 9:23–24: "Thus, says the LORD, 'Let not the wise man glory in his wisdom, let not the mighty man glory in his might, nor let the rich man glory in his riches; but let him who glories glory in this, that he understands and knows Me, that I am the LORD, exercising lovingkindness, judgment, and righteousness in the earth. For in these I delight', says the LORD." This is what the Lord delights in. This is the heart of God: for us to know Him and to understand Him and to boast in that reality. Our hope is not in our wisdom or the wisdom of other people. It is not in our own strength as a nation. It's not in our military might. Our strength is not in our economy. It's not in the stock market. It is in knowing and understanding the Lord our Creator. This reminds me of the hymn that goes, "My hope is built on nothing less than Jesus' blood and righteousness. I dare not trust the sweetest frame, but wholly lean on Jesus' name. On Christ the solid rock I stand, all other ground is sinking sand." Be praying for our nation, be praying for the church, be praying for believers. That we will have the heart of God, and we will speak truth to this nation out of love, compassion, and a redemptive heart.

Questions for Reflection and Discussion

1. In what should people boast according to verses 23–24?
    a. The wise boast in their wisdom.
    b. The mighty boast in their strength.
    c. The rich boast in their riches.
    d. The humble boast in understanding and knowing the Lord.

2. What do you think the difference is between mere physical circumcision and true spiritual circumcision of the heart (compare vv. 25–26 with Rom. 2:28–29)?

Notes on Today's Bible Reading

— DAY 10 —

Today's Reading: Jeremiah 10

Verse of the Day

> "For the customs of the peoples are futile; for one cuts a tree from the forest, the work of the hands of the workman, with the ax. They decorate it with silver and gold; they fasten it with nails and hammers so that it will not topple."
>
> *Jeremiah 10:3–4*

Please read the entire Scripture selection in your own Bible and highlight or underline verses that stand out to you before you read the observations and engage the questions below.

Have you ever heard the country saying, "That guy is as dumb as a post" or "dumb as a rock"? Basically, that saying questions the intelligence of another person, comparing their brain with an inanimate object—a piece of wood or a stone. Well that was what God was saying about His people who were crafting and worshipping idols. It's not only dumb to do that, but also the idolater becomes like the object they worship.

In chapter 10, Jeremiah returns to a charge that was common in the book of God's law, namely don't follow the practices of the pagans (see vv. 2–3a; also see Deut. 12:1–4; 29–31). In fact, God said their ways were "futile." To borrow from Paul, "[A]lthough they knew God, they did not glorify Him as God, nor were thankful, but became futile in their thoughts, and their foolish hearts were darkened. Professing to be wise, they became fools, and changed the glory of the incorruptible God into an image made like corruptible man—and birds and four-footed animals and creeping things" (Rom. 1:21–23). God tells us here that in their futility His people turned to idolatry, and His description of their practice drips with satire, much like the prophet Isaiah did in a previous generation (see Isa. 44:9–20).

God through Jeremiah describes in detail the futile and foolish production, beautification, and stabilization of an idol. First there is the *production* of the idol. Look at 10:3b: "For one cuts a tree from the forest, the work of the hands of the workman, with the ax." Production starts with a piece of wood or other inanimate object. An idol is essentially the "work of our own hands." We reject our Creator by trying to create our own god. An idol is a product of the imagination of sinful hearts and crafted by fallible hands. Later Jeremiah speaks of the professionals involved in production, the "craftsman" and the "metalsmith," describing the product as the "work of skillful men" (v. 9). Next comes the *beautification* of the idol. Precious metals are imported (v. 9), and these craftsmen take the piece of wood and "decorate it with silver and gold" (v. 4a), and they dress it up: "Blue and purple are their clothing" (v. 9). Then comes the *stabilization* of the idol: "They fasten it with nails and hammers so that it will not topple." (v. 4b). Do you see the satire, the irony in idolatry? You have to make the idol, dress it up, and make it look nice, then must secure it so it doesn't fall down. And *that* is what people fall down before and worship? Just to drive it home, look at verse 5: "They are upright, like a palm tree, and they cannot speak; they must be carried, because they cannot go by themselves. Do not be afraid of them, for they cannot do evil, nor can they do any good." Idolatry is futile and foolish.

In our contemporary and cynical culture, we profess to be much more sophisticated than that. No one I know literally bows down before a wooden or stone idol like they did Jeremiah's day. Yet our generation has its own idols just the same. People worship the creation rather than the Creator. People worship pleasure and possessions instead of the Giver of every good and perfect gift. People worship the god of self instead of the Savior. Indeed, they worship a host of false gods with no less devotion than these ancient Jews. At the end of the day, it is just as futile and foolish. In fact, Jeremiah punctuates that point in verse 8: "But they are altogether dull-hearted and foolish; a wooden idol is a worthless doctrine."

Then Jeremiah makes the stark contrast between these dumb, do-nothing idols and the almighty God. In fact, he can't help himself because, in the middle of his description of idol worship, the prophet breaks out in praise: "Inasmuch as there is none like You, O LORD (You are great, and Your name is great in might), who would not fear You, O King of the nations? For this is Your rightful due. For among all the wise men of the nations, and in all their kingdoms, there is none like You" (vv. 6–7). He continues it in verses 12–13: "He has made the earth by His power, He has established the world by His wisdom, and has stretched out the heavens at His discretion. When He utters His voice, there is a multitude of waters in the heavens: 'And He causes the vapors to ascend from the ends of the earth. He makes lightning for the rain, He brings the wind out of His treasuries.'" The bottom line? There is no comparison between the one true God and all these pathetic pretenders. Jeremiah closes with this declaration in verse 16: "The Portion of Jacob is not like them, for He is the Maker of all things, and Israel is the tribe of His inheritance; the LORD of hosts is His name."

Again, modern Americans would scoff at the thought of bowing down to an idol of wood or stone. Yet many worship idols of their own making just the same. While our current idols may be less crude and a bit more sophisticated, they are still idols. In fact, any rival to God is an idol. To what or to whom are you giving the lion's share of your time, your affection, your devotion, your finances, and so forth? Show me that person, passion, or possession, and I will show you your god. Jeremiah 10 offers an excellent opportunity to make a spiritual assessment, call us to repentance, and renew our allegiance to the one true and living God, the Maker of heaven and earth.

Questions for Reflection and Discussion

1. To what does God compare worthless idols (see v. 5)?

2. What were some expressions Jeremiah used of the Lord when contrasting His attributes with worthless idols (see vv. 6–16)?

Notes on Today's Bible Reading

— DAY 11 —

Today's Reading: Jeremiah 11

Verse of the Day

> And the LORD said to me, "A conspiracy has been found among the men of Judah and among the inhabitants of Jerusalem."
>
> *Jeremiah 11:9*

Please read the entire Scripture selection in your own Bible and highlight or underline verses that stand out to you before you read the observations and engage the questions below.

Some things never change. In this chapter, Jeremiah faced the cancel culture for revealing a conspiracy. What was the conspiracy? We'll talk about it. Our key verse is verse 9, "And the LORD said to me, 'A conspiracy has been found among the men of Judah and among the inhabitants of Jerusalem.'" Now, let me give you the context for this verse. This message comes during the reign of King Jehoiakim. This was after the death of Josiah. The temple had been repaired, and during that time, the Word of God, the law of Moses, was discovered in the temple. It was read to the people, and the covenant was renewed. They found the law and realized they weren't keeping it. So Josiah led in a renewal of the covenant among the people. You can read more about it in 2 Kings 23.

The reforms of Josiah and the discovery of the Word did bring about a revival of sorts. But as we will see from Jeremiah's message here and going forward, the revival was superficial. So let's begin in Jeremiah 11:1–4: "The word that came to Jeremiah from the LORD, saying, 'Hear the words of this covenant, and speak to the men of Judah and to the inhabitants of Jerusalem; and say to them, "Thus says the LORD God of Israel: 'Cursed is the man who does not obey the words of this covenant which I commanded your fathers in the day I brought them out of the land of Egypt, from the iron furnace, saying, "Obey My voice, and do according to all that I command you; so shall you be My people, and I will be your God."'"

You see, the relationship is this: "I'll be your God. You obey me, I will be your God, and you'll be my people." Look at verses 5–6: "'that I may establish the oath which I have sworn to your fathers, to give them "a land flowing with milk and honey," as it is this day.'" They were in the promised land. "And I answered and said, 'So be it, LORD.' Then the LORD said to me, 'Proclaim all these words in the cities of Judah and in the streets of Jerusalem, saying: "Hear the words of this covenant and do them."'" They had voluntarily renewed the covenant, but yet they weren't doing it. Verses 7–10:

> "For I earnestly exhorted your fathers in the day I brought them up out of the land of Egypt, until this day, rising early and exhorting, saying, 'Obey My voice.' Yet they did not obey or incline their ear, but everyone followed the dictates of his evil heart; therefore I will bring upon them all the words of this covenant, which I commanded them to do, but which they have not done." And the LORD said to me, "A conspiracy has been found among the men of Judah and among the inhabitants of Jerusalem. They have turned back to the iniquities of their forefathers who refused to hear My words, and they have gone after other gods to serve them; the house of Israel and the house of Judah have broken My covenant which I made with their fathers."

Here's the conspiracy: despite the fact they had renewed the covenant and experienced a revival of sorts—after the reform efforts of Josiah cleaning out the temple and tearing down the high places and all the idolatry—we read in previous chapters, people were going back to the temple, but they were still worshipping their idols. Additionally, they wanted the blessings, but they didn't want to obey the voice of God. They refused to listen to God. They refused to hear Him. They refused to obey Him. So hearing is not just, "Oh, I heard that." It's yielding to it and obeying it. They refused to follow God; they traded the truth for a lie. That's what their fathers did. They traded the one true God for idols made by their own hands.

Note here, there is a warning for those to whom God has extended His mercy. Look at verse 11: "Therefore thus says the LORD" 'Behold, I will surely bring calamity on them which they will not be able to escape; and though they cry out to Me, I will not listen to them.'" They enjoyed the blessings of the covenant but did not keep the covenant. As a result, the consequences would come. In fact, we see it over in Deuteronomy 11 where their forefathers did it. And then Judah renewed this during Josiah's reign when the law was found. God says this, "There comes a point. I won't listen anymore." Now, that is not a place where we want to be, where God says, "I've had enough."

So that's the conspiracy. But as Jeremiah reveals this conspiracy, it brings out the cancel culture, which is the same as the cancel culture we see today. I mean, it's not new. Look at how they respond to Jeremiah in 11:18–20:

> Now the LORD gave me knowledge of it, and I know it; for You showed me their doings. But I was like a docile lamb brought to the slaughter; and I did not know that they had devised schemes against me saying, "Let us destroy the tree with its fruit [meaning the prophet who speaks the prophecies] and let us cut him off from the land of the living, that his name may be remembered no more." But, O LORD of hosts, You who judge righteously, testing the mind and the heart, let me see Your vengeance on them, for to you I have revealed my cause.

Now verses 21–23: "Therefore thus says the LORD concerning the men of Anathoth who seek your life, saying, 'Do not prophesy in the name of the LORD, lest you die by our hand'—therefore thus says the LORD of hosts: 'Behold, I will punish them. The young men shall die by the sword, their sons and their daughters shall die by famine; and there shall be no remnant of them, for I will bring catastrophe on the men of Anathoth, even the year of their punishment.'" Now these are the men of his own town. He grew up with them. They were the closest to him. They knew him, yet they wanted to cancel him. Now there is a passage that is almost universally known from the Bible. It's John 3:16. But what comes after it is not so well known. Look at John 3:17–20.

> For God did not send His Son into the world to condemn the world, but that the world through Him might be saved. He who believes in Him is not condemned; but he who does not believe is condemned already, because he has not believed in the name of the only begotten Son of God. And this is the condemnation, that the light has come into the world, and men loved darkness rather than light, because their deeds were evil. For everyone practicing evil hates the light and does not come to the light, lest his deeds should be exposed.

You see, the cancel culture—whether it's today or in Jeremiah's day or in the day of Jesus—has always loved the darkness and does not want their deeds to be made known. Jeremiah revealed the conspiracy, and they responded by wanting to silence him. But look at what we see repeatedly through the book of Jeremiah. God assures Jeremiah that He is with him and the cancel culture will not succeed against him. And Jesus assures His followers the same thing in Matthew 28:19–20 in the Great Commission. He says, "Go therefore and make disciples of all the nations, baptizing them in the name of the Father and of the Son and of the Holy Spirit, teaching them to observe all things that I have commanded you; and lo, I am with you always, even to the end of the age."

Questions for Reflection and Discussion

1. God asked Jeremiah to remind His people of what important era in their history (vv. 1–5)?

2. How did Jeremiah find out about the plot on his life (vv. 18–20)?
   a. Local gossip
   b. Magic eight ball
   c. Psychic friends network
   d. God's revealed Word

Notes on Today's Bible Reading

— DAY 12 —

Today's Reading: Jeremiah 12–13

Verse of the Day

> "If you have run with the footmen, and they have wearied you, then how can you contend with horses? And if in the land of peace, in which you trusted, they wearied you, then how will you do in the floodplain of the Jordan?"
>
> *Jeremiah 12:5*

Please read the entire Scripture selection in your own Bible and highlight or underline verses that stand out to you before you read the observations and engage the questions below.

By this point in the timeline of Jeremiah's prophecy, King Josiah was gone, dying an untimely death based on an unwise decision to take on King Necho of Egypt in battle (see 2 Chron. 35:20–24). Josiah was a good king who brought about reform, but the effects of the short-lived revival were diminishing as the people continued in their idolatry. So the opposition to the prophetic message of Jeremiah was building toward him for calling the people to repent and return to God. And quite frankly, it's beginning to wear on Jeremiah, and we see that. Today's reading encompasses chapters 12–13, but we will look at chapter 13 along with chapter 19.

Let's start by looking at 12:1–4.

> Righteous are You, O Lord, when I plead with You; yet let me talk with You about Your judgments. Why does the way of the

> wicked prosper? Why are those happy who deal so treacherously? You have planted them, yes, they have taken root; they grow, yes, they bear fruit. You are near in their mouths but far from their mind. But You, O Lord, know me; You have seen me, and You have tested my heart toward You. Pull them out like sheep for the slaughter, and prepare them for the day of slaughter. How long will the land mourn, and the herbs of every field wither? The beasts and birds are consumed, for the wickedness of those who dwell there, because they said, "He will not see our final end."

In verses 5–6, God responded to Jeremiah. "'If you have run with the footmen, and they have wearied you, then how can you contend with horses? And if in the land of peace, in which you trusted, they wearied you, then how will you do in the floodplain of the Jordan? For even your brothers, the house of your father, even they have dealt treacherously with you; yes, they have called a multitude after you. Do not believe them, even though they speak smooth words to you.'"

Have you ever asked the question, Why does the way of the wicked prosper? Jeremiah was not the first to ask that question, and I'm sure he won't be the last. In Psalm 94:2–5, the psalmist asked that question: "Rise up, O Judge of the earth; render punishment to the proud. Lord, how long with the wicked, how long will the wicked triumph? They utter speech, and speak insolent things; all the workers of iniquity boast in themselves. They break in pieces your people, O Lord, and afflict your heritage." Have you ever asked that question? "Lord, why do those prosper who give you lip service but whose hearts are far from you? They don't give a second thought about your truth."

I recall back during my days in the state legislature, debating legislation, there were those who were really advocating for things that run completely counter to the Word of God and to His truth about morality. And they would stand up and quote Scripture, saying, "'He who is without sin among you, let him throw a stone at her first" (see John 8:7). You see, the Lord was on their lips, the Word of God, but He was not in their minds and in their hearts. They would use the

Word of God. And so this is where Jeremiah was. The people were going through the motions. They had renewed the covenant, but their minds were far from God. They were not living according to the truth. So Jeremiah asked that question respectfully of God.

And look at God's reply: "If you have run with the footmen, and they have wearied you, then how can you contend with horses? And if in the land of peace, in which you trusted, they wearied you, then how will you do in the floodplain of the Jordan?" God listened patiently to Jeremiah then told him he hadn't seen anything yet. I'm not going to minimize what Jeremiah was feeling. I mean, we talked about this before. He faced the cancel culture. His family, friends, the people he grew up with had turned against him. He was isolated, marginalized. He was alone. And he was weary. It's difficult to stand in the face of the broader culture and stand alone. He was tired of contending with the people who were rejecting God. Because he was following God, he had the ability to see the end result of their sin, so he was also burdened for his people. He talked about the land. "How long would the land mourn?" You see, sin has a consequence upon the land. He was concerned about the animals. He was concerned about the environment. And he was also concerned about those people who were not leading. They were only sheep, and they were following. He knew what the end result would be, and so his heart was burdened. He asked, "How long will the wicked prosper?" How long will those who lead the people in the wrong way continue to prosper?

There's an English preacher and theologian I quote from time to time, Matthew Henry. He wrote, "While we are in this world, we must expect troubles and difficulties. Our life is a race, a warfare. We are in danger of being run down."[2] This is exactly what Jesus told us to be prepared for. John 16:33 says, "These things I have spoken to you, that in Me you may have peace. In the world you will have tribulation; but be of good cheer, I have overcome the world." You're going to face difficulty if you live for Jesus Christ.

There's been a time in the history of this country when there was a predominant climate, morally and spiritually, in which it was accepted to be a Christian. In fact, most wanted to be that way. I think that was similar to the early days of the revival Josiah led. They were kind of going through the motions, but some of it was legitimate. Then it turned. I think that's where we are in America today. Christianity is mocked, and it's a wearisome environment to stand for Jesus Christ. It can cost you. But what the Lord is saying here is, "In this world, you're going to have tribulation, but in me you'll have peace." So what does that mean? We have to press into God. We need to spend time in God's Word. That's why I encourage you to continue in the Stand on the Word Bible reading plan because it will help you realize you're not alone. Jeremiah faced difficulty, but God was with him. Commentator Matthew Henry also said, "God's usual method being to begin with smaller trials is to our wisdom to expect greater than any we have yet met with."[3] Basically, God uses these small things to prepare us for greater challenges that are going to come our way. Why should we want to be prepared? For the glory of God.

Through your life as you stand with confidence and peace through Christ in the midst of tribulation, difficulty, and opposition, it is a witness to a lost and dying world. And Jeremiah was to continue to stand for the truth and not shrink back. Now, that takes me to a third point here. God's reply to the question, How long will the wicked prosper? Is, "Look, you haven't seen anything yet." So how should we respond? Again, I go back to the words of Jesus when He calls people to follow Him in Luke 9:23–25: "Then He said to them all, 'If anyone desires to come after Me, let him deny himself, and take up his cross daily, and follow Me. For whoever desires to save his life will lose it, but whoever loses his life for My sake will save it. For what profit is it to a man if he gains the whole world, and is himself destroyed or lost?"

See, Jesus called us. He told us we are to deny ourselves. If we are to follow Him, daily we must deny ourselves, take up our cross, which is an instrument of death, and follow him. You see, we're called to something greater than ourselves, and we have to lay down our lives. We have to expect tribulation and opposition, but in Christ we have peace. So today, I encourage you to continue to read through God's Word and remember you're not alone. There have been others who have faced challenges before, but we need to draw close to the

Lord Jesus Christ, not withdrawing from the world but finding our strength and our hope and our peace in Jesus Christ alone.

Questions for Reflection and Discussion

1. With a challenge in 12:5, God replies to Jeremiah's question about why the way of the wicked prospers. Which statement below best reflects that challenge?

   a. If you can't stand the heat, get out of the kitchen.
   b. If you can't run with the big dogs, stay on the porch.
   c. If you can't keep up with the infantry, how will you run with the cavalry?
   d. None of the above.

2. What did God tell Jeremiah to do with his loincloth (underwear) in 13?

Notes on Today's Bible Reading

— DAY 13 —

Today's Reading: Jeremiah 14

Verse of the Day

> O Lord, though our iniquities testify against us, do it for Your name's sake; for our backslidings are many, we have sinned against You.
>
> *Jeremiah 14:7*

Please read the entire Scripture selection in your own Bible and highlight or underline verses that stand out to you before you read the observations and engage the questions below.

Have you ever heard the saying: "Too little, too late"? Well, that sums up what God said to His wayward and idolatrous people in Jeremiah 14. Because they were suffering the consequences of their sin, they decided now it is time to repent. Let's see how God responded and how the prophet Jeremiah interceded.

At the beginning of the chapter, we find that God's disciplinary judgment came in the form of a withering drought that was devastating for humans, animals, and crops (vv. 1–6). Consequently, the people of Judah cried out to God in verses 7–9. Look at verse 7: "O Lord, though our iniquities testify against us, do it for Your name's sake; for our backslidings are many, we have sinned against You." While this seems to be a step in the right direction, it is really "too little, too late." It is sort of like dealing with a disobedient child, who gets warning after warning for bad behavior, but when the punishment starts, it is only then that child suddenly realizes the need to confess and course-correct in order to get relief. When the begging starts, the hope is that the punishment will stop. That is what God's people were doing here. They wanted relief from the consequences without a genuine change of heart. Again, their confession was "too little, too late."

Well, God is having none of it. He declared in verse 10, "Thus says the LORD to this people: 'Thus they have loved to wander; they have not restrained their feet. Therefore the LORD does not accept them; He will remember their iniquity now, and punish their sins.'" In fact, God told Jeremiah for the third time, "'Do not pray for this people'" (v. 11; see also 7:16; 11:14). He added in verse 12, "'When they fast, I will not hear their cry; and when they offer burnt offering and grain offering, I will not accept them. But I will consume them by the sword, by the famine, and by the pestilence.'"

It didn't help matters that Jeremiah's rivals, the false prophets were prophesying "'lies in My name. I have not sent them, commanded them, nor spoken to them; they prophesy to you a false vision, [c]divination, a worthless thing, and the deceit of their heart'" (v. 14). They lied to the people, claiming, "'Sword and famine shall not be in this land.'" God pronounced judgment on them: "'By sword and famine those prophets shall be consumed!" (v. 15), and the people who listened to them, who will be victims of "famine and sword; they will have no one to bury them—them nor their wives, their sons nor their daughters—for I will pour their wickedness on them'" (v. 16).

In light of this bleak situation, the prophet Jeremiah wept over his people (v. 17) and pressed the issue with God: "Have You utterly rejected Judah? Has Your soul loathed Zion? Why have you stricken us so that there is no healing for us?" (v. 19). Indeed, he intercedes for them in verse 20: "We acknowledge, O LORD, our wickedness and the iniquity of our fathers, for we have sinned against you." Though God told Jeremiah not to pray for them, the prophet continued to do so: "Do not abhor us, for Your name's sake; do not disgrace the throne of Your glory. Remember, do not break Your covenant with us. Are there any among the idols of the nations that can cause rain? Or can the heavens give showers? Are You not He, O LORD our God? Therefore we will wait for You, since You have made all these" (vv. 21–22).

What was happening in Jeremiah's day seems all too familiar. Like Judah, America seems bent on inviting God's judgment with our bad behavior. And like Judah, we occasionally "rediscover our religion" and cry out to God when we feel the consequences of our sin. Like the false prophets, plenty of people-pleasing, woke ministers in our churches comfort us rather than confront us in our sin with biblical preaching. Yet like Jeremiah, we must be dedicated to speak God's truth in love to this generation, while interceding and pleading with God on behalf for our nation. Let's pray for a genuine return to God in America marked by humble repentance. And if it comes, let's pray that, unlike it was with Judah, it is not "too little, too late" for America.

Questions for Reflection and Discussion

1. On what basis did Jeremiah plead for God's intervention and what was God's reply in verses 7–12?

2. What judgment did God pronounce on the "lying prophets" who were spreading fake messages and giving false hope (see vv. 13–16)?

Notes on Today's Bible Reading

— DAY 14 —

Today's Reading: Jeremiah 15

Verse of the Day

> O Lord, You know; remember me and visit me, and take vengeance for me on my persecutors. In Your enduring patience, do not take me away. Know that for Your sake I have suffered rebuke.
>
> *Jeremiah 15:15*

Please read the entire Scripture selection in your own Bible and highlight or underline verses that stand out to you before you read the observations and engage the questions below.

Weary of the cancel culture and tempted to quit? So was Jeremiah as we will see later in chapter 15. This chapter can be separated into four major components: the cause, the complaint, the challenge, and the promise. The first nine verses are a continuation of the message from chapter 14. And once again, we read of the pending judgment and the suffering that will follow because it's described in great detail. Now, in the remaining portion of the chapter, we find a weary prophet complaining that God had abandoned him then we find God's response.

So we are going to start with the first nine verses because in this we see the cause. Why is this judgment coming? Well, we've heard over and over again about the sins of the people and their refusal to repent, to turn away from their idolatry and follow the Lord. Remember, Josiah brought about a reform and cleansed the temple. The people were back worshipping, but they were continuing in their idolatry. And here the Lord pointed to the root cause of the coming judgment in verse 4: "'I will hand them over to trouble to all the kingdoms of the earth, because of Manasseh the son of Hezekiah, king of Judah, for what he did in Jerusalem.'" What did he do? We see the answer over in 2 Chronicles 33:9: "So Manasseh seduced Jerusalem and the inhabitants of Jerusalem to do more evil than the nations whom the Lord had destroyed before the children of Israel." Manasseh was not only a bad king; he was a really bad king. He reigned for fifty-two years. His imprint upon the nation was irrefutable, and he led the people into doing more evil than the nations the Scripture says God spewed out of the land because of the abominations they had been involved in.

In 2 Kings 24:3–4 we read this, "Surely at the commandment of the Lord this came upon Judah, to remove them from His sight because of the sins of Manasseh, according to all that he had done, and also because of the innocent blood that he had shed; for he had filled Jerusalem with innocent blood, which the Lord would not pardon." See God waited until the third and fourth generations to punish the nation for the sins of Manasseh. I believe it was because He was providing an opportunity for His people to truly repent. Now, the sins of Manasseh were idolatry. He put up idols everywhere, including in the temple of God. And this was continuing again; despite the reform efforts of Josiah, they simply added the rituals of their covenantal relationship with God. They were having the feast again. They were going to the temple, but they were still engaging in their idolatry. Consequently, His judgment was coming.

Now in regard to Manasseh, many scholars think the blood he shed in the streets refers to him persecuting and killing the prophets of God. The innocent blood was that of the prophets. Those people who were speaking the truth of God were killed. This hostility toward the prophets continued as we see the way Jeremiah was persecuted. And then, of course, Manasseh led the people in sacrificing their children to idols, to Molech. So here's something that we should take note of. At the end of Manasseh's life, after he had been taken away and imprisoned by the king of Assyria, he repented of his sins. The Bible actually says that he knew that the Lord was God (see 2 Chron. 33:12–13). Now, this would suggest that his sins were pardoned because he repented and the Scripture points that out. The problem is these sins had become a national sin. He seduced the people into committing these sins. This became a part of who they were as a people. And they had not repented of these and continued in their sin.

Now, consider where this leaves America because we've pushed God aside. We've taken Him out of our schools, we've pushed Him out of the public square, and those who speak and live the truth of God are in many cases actually punished by their own government. And, of course, the sacrificing of the innocent continues. It's quite sobering!

Now, let's move to the second portion of this chapter and first look at the complaint. This is Jeremiah's complaint in verses 15–18.

> O Lord, You know; remember me and visit me, and take vengeance for me on my persecutors. In Your enduring patience, do not take me away. Know that for Your sake I have suffered rebuke. Your words were found, and I ate them, and Your word was to me the joy and rejoicing of my heart; for I am called by Your name, O Lord God of hosts. I did not sit in the assembly of the mockers, nor did I rejoice; I sat alone because of Your hand, for You have filled me with indignation. Why is my pain perpetual and my wound incurable, which refuses to be healed? Will You surely be to me like an unreliable stream, as waters that fail?

Basically, Jeremiah said, "Lord, I've stood up for you. I've spoken your words. Now I'm alone. The cancel culture has targeted me. But where are you? You're like an unreliable stream to me." Now, this sounds like Elijah after his confrontation with the prophets of Baal and the queen of cancel culture, Jezebel, came after him. Trust me, when you stand for the Lord, these times will come. But I think Jeremiah crossed the line here. Look at God's response in verse 19, which is the challenge, "Therefore thus says the Lord, 'If you return, then I will bring you back; you shall stand before Me; if you take out the precious from the vile, you shall be as My mouth. Let them return to you, but you must not return to them.'" In other words, "You've crossed over the line. Your eyes and focus are so much on those who oppose you, you've allowed them to condition and guide your thinking. You're more influenced by them than they are influenced by you. Return to Me, get your focus straight, get your eyes on Me."

Now in verses 20–21 we see the promise, "'And I will make you to this people a fortified bronze wall; and they will fight against you, but they shall not prevail against you; for I am with you to save you and deliver you,' says the Lord. 'I will deliver you from the hand of the wicked, and I will redeem you from the grip of the terrible.'" God repeats His promise that He gave Jeremiah at his commissioning back in 1:18–19, "'For behold, I have made you this day a fortified city and an iron pillar, and bronze walls against the whole land—against the kings of Judah, against its princes, against its priests, and against the people of the land. They will fight against you, but they shall not prevail against you. For I am with you,' says the Lord, 'to deliver you.'" You know, sometimes we just need to be reminded of God's promises and we need to stand in His strength. In Ephesians 6:10, Paul says, "be strong in the Lord and in the power of His might." That's our strength. We need to stand close to the Lord. If we're going to stand for the Lord, we need to stand upon his word and return to His promises. And just as we need to be reminded of His promises, we need to be reminded that yesterday's obedience does not secure today's blessings. We need to walk with the Lord each and every day in humble obedience before Him.

Questions for Reflection and Discussion

1. What two great Old Testament personalities did God say He would not even listen to if they tried to intercede on behalf of Judah (see v. 1)?

2. What conditional promises did God offer to Jeremiah after he essentially accused the Lord of letting him down in verse 18 (see 15:19–21)?

   a. If you return, I will restore you.
   b. If you utter worthy, not worthless words, you will be my spokesman.

c. I will make you a fortified wall to this people; they will fight against you but will not prevail.
d. I will save you from the hands of the wicked and from the grasp of the cruel.
e. All of the above.

Notes on Today's Bible Reading

— DAY 15 —

Today's Reading: Jeremiah 16

Verse of the Day

> "Therefore behold, I will this once cause them to know, I will cause them to know My hand and My might; and they shall know that My name is the Lord."
>
> *Jeremiah 16:21*

Please read the entire Scripture selection in your own Bible and highlight or underline verses that stand out to you before you read the observations and engage the questions below.

What is God's purpose in punishing and judging His people? The answer to that question can be found in Jeremiah 16. By now, you're probably thinking this message from Jeremiah is so clear: Judgment is coming, and they're going to be punished for their sins. Over and over we're seeing the same thing repeated: idolatry, wickedness, repentance, turning back to God. You know, it kind of reminds me of a father with kids in the back of the car acting up, present company included. As he's driving down the road, he tells the kids, "If you don't straighten up, I'm going to pull over." And of course, he's hoping that just the threat of punishment is going to be enough to get them to straighten up. But eventually he must find a place to pull over. In fact, our kids got pretty proficient at identifying what they called spanking places alongside the road. Well, here's God, basically saying, "Straighten up or I'm going to pull over."

So, the question is, Why was God slow to pull over? We read the reason in 2 Peter 3:9: "The Lord is not slack concerning His promise, as some count slackness, but is longsuffering toward us, not willing that any should perish but that all should come to repentance." Now there were those in Jeremiah's day, just as there are in our day, who didn't believe the words of God to be true. They were so focused on the things of this world and what they saw, felt, and touched that they were deceived into thinking it was permanent and nothing could take it away. Well, we're going to see through this chapter, God trying to get the attention of His people. This short chapter, which only contains twenty-one verses, can be broken into four parts, but I'm only going to read some of the highlights.

Let's start with part 1, the *restrictions* on Jeremiah. That's the first nine verses where he's told not to marry or have children. He is not to participate in mourning for the dead or in joyous occasions. And the question is why? Well the restrictions, I believe, were both practical and prophetic. First, he was going to live through the time of the judgment when the children of Israel were carried away into Babylon. And so not having a wife and children, he could stay focused on his mission from God and not be concerned about their well-being—as you read in these first nine verses, it's going to be really, really bad. Secondly, it was prophetic. They're going through life, thinking nothing's going to happen, and here's this guy who's countercultural. He was single. That's unusual. He was not mourning the dead. That's unusual. He was not joining in joyous celebrations. So both in his words and his actions he was able to speak prophetically to the seriousness of the impending judgment. That's the first part.

The second part is a *restatement* of the indictment against Judah in verses 10–11: "'And it shall be, when you show this people all these words, and they say to you, "Why has the Lord pronounced all this great disaster against us? Or what is our iniquity? Or what is our sin that we have committed against the Lord our God?" then you shall say to them, "Because your fathers have forsaken Me," says the Lord; "they have walked after other gods and have served them and worshiped them, and have forsaken Me and not kept My law."'" Well, they said,

"That's just our fathers." But look at verses 12–13: "'And you have done worse than your fathers, for behold, each one follows the dictates of his own evil heart, so that no one listens to Me. Therefore I will cast you out of this land into a land that you do not know, neither you nor your fathers.'" Remember, we see this over and over. God told them at the very beginning, when He brought them into the land, that if they followed the ways of the previous inhabitants of the land, He would do the same thing to them. He would hurl them out. He would spew them out of the land. And then the final verse or final portion of verse 13 says, "and there you shall serve other gods day and night, where I will not show you favor.'" That's quite a significant thing. You see, it's the favor of God that was upon them. It was not their own ability. They came from nothing, but it was the favor of God. And so I think even in America, what has made it an exceptional, great nation in the past has been the favor of God. What we need is the favor of God. Well, how do you get the favor of God? The favor of God is upon those who follow God, who are in fellowship with God, who obey God. "If you love me," Jesus said, "you'll keep my commandments." We need the favor of God upon our lives. We need the favor of God upon our families. We need the favor of God upon our churches. We need the favor of God upon our nation. And that comes through obedience to God.

Now let's jump over to verse 17 because in verses 17–18 He continues in why this judgment is coming in this indictment. He said, "For My eyes are on all their ways; they are not hidden from My face, nor is their iniquity hidden from My eyes." You can't hide anything from God. He sees it. And then verse 18: "And first I will repay double for their iniquity and their sin, because they have defiled My land; they have filled My inheritance with the carcasses of their detestable and abominable idols." It comes back to their idolatry, putting other things first, and, of course, we've already talked about what was included in this idolatry. There was sexual immorality and even the sacrificing of their children.

So we have the *restrictions* on the prophet. We have the *restatement* of the indictment. Then the third part is, we have the *restoration* promise. God is a God of mercy and hope. We're never beyond hope with God. As long as we have breath, there is hope. Verse 10, "And it shall be, when you show this people all these words, and they say to you, 'Why has the Lord pronounced all this great disaster against us? Or what is our iniquity? Or what is our sin that we have committed against the Lord our God?'" Again, that was the restatement of the indictment. But go to verses 14–15: "'Therefore behold, the days are coming,' says the LORD, 'that it shall no more be said, "The LORD lives who brought up the children of Israel from the land of Egypt," but, "The LORD lives who brought up the children of Israel from the land of the north and from all the lands where He had driven them." For I will bring them back into their land which I gave to their fathers.'" So He said, "Look, I'm going to be known, not as the one who brought you out of Egypt, but I'm going to be known as the God who brought you up out of the north country, out of the Babylonian captivity." But this speaks not only to the return of the Babylonian captivity but also to the end time gathering of the children of Israel back to their land.

Now, here's the fourth and final part of this chapter: the *reformation* of sinners as a result of God's judgment. Proverbs 19:25 says, "Strike a scoffer, and the simple will become wary; rebuke one who has understanding, and he will discern knowledge." Look what it says in Jeremiah 16:19–20: "O LORD, my strength and my fortress, my refuge in the day of affliction, the Gentiles shall come to You from the ends of the earth and say, 'Surely our fathers have inherited lies, worthlessness and unprofitable things.' Will a man make gods for himself, which are not gods?" Or in other words, a better translation of that is, "Shall man make gods though men themselves are not gods?" So what he is saying is that, through what is happening here, the punishment is going to make people's ears tingle when they hear it. It's going to be so bad they will realize man can't make their own gods. And we saw this after the Babylonian captivity where even the Gentiles came to be a part of worshipping the one true God. Look at Jeremiah 16:21: "'Therefore, behold, I will this once cause them to know, I will cause them to know My hand and My might; and they shall know that My name is the LORD.'" This brings us back to our opening question, What is God's purpose in punishing and judging His people? The answer is in the very last sentence of this chapter: "And they shall know that My name is the LORD." It all comes back to the glory of God, that men, women, and children will know Him, their Creator, and have a relationship with Him in such a way as they worship and they honor Him.

Questions for Reflection and Discussion

1. What normal life experiences did God tell Jeremiah to abstain from in verses 1–9?

  a. Marriage and having kids
  b. Going to funerals
  c. Participating in celebrations
  d. All of the above

2. Looking to the future deliverance from Babylonian captivity, God promised it would eclipse what great deliverance in His people's past?

Notes on Today's Bible Reading

— DAY 16 —

Today's Reading: Jeremiah 17

Verse of the Day

> "Blessed is the man who trusts in the LORD, and whose hope is the LORD."
>
> *Jeremiah 17:7*

Please read the entire Scripture selection in your own Bible and highlight or underline verses that stand out to you before you read the observations and engage the questions below.

This chapter begins with a restatement of what was at the heart of Judah's sin, its idolatry, and the pending judgment that God said was coming as a result. The children followed in the footsteps of their parents by engaging in the worship of idols, primarily as it talks about in this passage. They worshipped Asherah, a Canaanite fertility goddess. This idolatry was not just bowing down to a wooden pole, but it included sexual immorality. Consequently, orgies took place in groves on top of hills. So we're going to read about part of this.

Let's begin in Jeremiah 17:1: "The sin of Judah is written with a pen of iron; with the point of a diamond it is engraved on the tablet of their heart, and on the horns of your altars." In other words, this sin was indelibly inscribed on their hearts. This was their identity; it was who they were. It was defining, unfortunately. Verses 2–4: "'while their children remember their altars and their wooden images by the green trees on the high hills. O My mountain in the field, I will give as plunder your wealth, all your treasures, and your high places of sin within all your borders. And you, even yourself, shall let go of your heritage which I gave you; and I will cause you to serve your enemies in the land which you do not know; for you have kindled a fire in My anger which shall burn forever.'" They had engaged in idolatry. And oftentimes, as they prospered, God blessed them in the promised land, but then they began to stray; they began to engage in all of these sinful activities of idolatry and sexual immorality. And it's interesting, as we've already read, but the whole family would do it. The wives made cakes, the kids gathered the sticks to bake those cakes. And the husbands gave them as sacrifices to these idols. And so, they were actually giving the very thing that God had given them to these idols. See they weren't only getting by, just having enough food to eat. They were blessed. So they were using this as a part of their idolatry. And that is just so offensive to the God who provides for us and blesses us. We turn around with what He has given us and use it to worship idols!

Let's go on to verses 5–8:

> Thus says the Lord: "Cursed is the man who trusts in man and makes flesh his strength, whose heart departs from the Lord. For he shall be like a shrub in the desert, and shall not see when good comes, but shall inhabit the parched places in the wilderness, in a salt land which is not inhabited. Blessed is the man who trusts in the Lord, and whose hope is the Lord. For he shall be like a tree planted by the waters, which spreads out its roots by the river, and will not fear when heat comes; but its leaf will be green, and will not be anxious in the year of drought, nor will cease from yielding fruit.

Now jump to verses 9–10: "'The heart is deceitful above all things, and desperately wicked; who can know it? I, the Lord, search the heart, I test the mind, even to give every man according to his ways, according to the fruit of his doings.'" I want us to see the curse here. The one who will be cursed is the one who puts his trust in man instead of God. And so instead of worshipping the Creator, we're putting our confidence in the created. This applies to us even today. This is humanism.

We think humans have the intellect, the ability, to solve all these problems and acknowledging the Creator is like a myth, a superstition. Well, when we put our trust in humans or we think we have the power within ourselves, we then depart from God. We see here, as read before, it's not that those in Jeremiah's day completely forgot God; they gave Him lip service, at most, but not the devotion of their hearts and lives. This is essentially practical atheism or being agnostic. It's recognizing God's existence but thinking we have to solve our own problems, that "man" is the ultimate source to which we owe our allegiance.

Look what Jesus said in Matthew 6:24: "'No one can serve two masters; for either he will hate the one and love the other, or else he will be loyal to the one and despise the other. You cannot serve God and mammon.'" Now, what does it mean to be cursed by God? I think it means that you're going to be miserable. You're going to be frustrated. You're going to be unfulfilled. How do I know that? Well, look what it says in Jeremiah 17:6: "For he shall be like a shrub in the desert, and shall not see when good comes, but shall inhabit the parched places in the wilderness, in a salt land which is not inhabited." This is a desert shrub without water. It's barren. It's just out there. It lacks purpose. And that's really what being cursed by God is. You're fearful, and in fact, God said it over in Exodus and Leviticus. He said, "I will put the fear of you in those who meet you if you obey me. But if you disobey me, I'm going to put fear of them in you." So fear is a part of being cursed, fearful of someone coming after you, fearful of losing what you have, fearful of not having what you need and being barren. You're not providing for others. I mean, as believers, we have purpose in our lives, and we provide hope and direction for others. But if God curses by God, you're barren and your life lacks purpose.

Let's look now at the blessed in Jeremiah 17:7: "'Blessed is the man who trusts in the LORD, and whose hope is the LORD.'" Now what leads to being blessed by God? He puts it clearly in verse 7: "trust in the LORD." You trust in Him, putting your confidence in God and His word and what He said He will do, rather than putting your confidence and strength in the wisdom and the strength of others. So we trust God even when others reject Him, just like Jeremiah trusted

Him. Psalm 20:7 says, "Some trust in chariots, and some in horses; but we will remember the name of the LORD our God." Then not only did they trust in the Lord, but they placed their hope in the Lord; their security was placed in God. And because He is outside of time and space, He is the Creator, we can have confidence when we anchor our lives to Him. Our hope is God. Our hope is not in God, our hope is God. Then finally, what does it mean to be blessed by God? Well, this is actually almost identical to what Psalm 1:3 says: "He shall be like a tree planted by the rivers of water, that brings forth its fruit in season, whose leaf also shall not wither; and whatever he does shall prosper." What a contrast to the one who is cursed. There's confidence. He is rooted, planted by the rivers of water. Rivers are constantly coming. His roots are there. There is a certainty of the necessities of life. He's going to have them, and he has purpose. His life's not going to wither. He's not going to have to worry about droughts. He's prosperous. Whatever he does will prosper or bring forth his fruit in season. That's what we want—to bring forth fruit in season. And think about it. Fruit is not for a tree to consume itself. The fruit of a tree is to bless others. So we are to be a blessing.

God has created us first and foremost to worship Him. Man's chief end is to glorify God and to enjoy Him forever. But He uses us. If we yield ourselves to Him, He allows us to be a part of what He is doing to reach and minister to the lives of others. He prospers us so we can be a blessing to others. Then that allows us to fulfill our purpose. Now we may not be successful in terms of success in the eyes of the world, but we'll be significant in the eyes of God because we are living in purpose.

Go to the end of Jeremiah 17, verses 19–27, where he focuses on the call for them to honor the Sabbath. What is that all about? Is this only legalism? No, it is actually tied to what we were just talking about. Routinely working on the Sabbath is a byproduct of not trusting in or obeying God. They were working on the Sabbath, which was driven by one of two things. One, they wanted more so they were therefore worshipping the creation over the Creator. They were worshipping the creation of their own hands, or they were fearful they would not have enough, which was a result of not trusting God and placing their hope in God. And so they were working. They had to work seven days a week in order to make ends meet. That sound familiar?

Maybe we need to step back and trust God. I think that is an element, and you know, from time to time in my life, I've had to wrestle with that of stepping back because there's so much to do. But honoring God on the Sabbath and just spending time in His Word, spending time with the family, attending church with other believers, resting, not just laying on the couch watching football. That's not what we're talking about here. We're talking about not engaging in the things we need, trusting in others, but engaging in things that allow us to honor God. How we spend our Sunday, our Sabbath, is a reflection of where we are putting our trust and whether we will be blessed or whether we will be cursed.

Questions for Reflection and Discussion

1. What did Jeremiah say was "deceitful above all things and desperately sick" (see vv. 9–10)?

2. When God gave Jeremiah a message to preach at the People's Gate in Jerusalem, which of the Ten Commandments was the focus (see vv. 19–27)?

Notes on Today's Bible Reading

— DAY 17 —

Today's Reading: Jeremiah 18

Verse of the Day

> "O house of Israel, can I not do with you as this potter?" says the LORD. "Look, as the clay is in the potter's hand, so are you in My hand, O house of Israel!"
>
> *Jeremiah 18:6*

Please read the entire Scripture selection in your own Bible and highlight or underline verses that stand out to you before you read the observations and engage the questions below.

Are you clay or Silly Putty? Jeremiah 18:6b says, "'Look, as the clay is in the potter's hand, so are you in My hand.'" That's the Lord speaking. So are you clay or Silly Putty? That is what we are going to look at today. But first, here is the context for this chapter. The people were refusing to listen to the words of the prophet of Jeremiah. Remember, we've gone through all of these different messages he'd given, warning them of impending judgment because of their sin of idolatry and everything associated with it. The Lord then began to give him sermon illustrations, so the people could "see" the message. Sometimes, the prophet Jeremiah was acting out these messages, as we will see in the next chapter. However, in chapter 18, it is more of a "show and tell" message with a visit to the potter's house.

Here we see the power of the potter, the power of the people, and the prayer of the prophet. Let's start by reading Jeremiah 18:1–12:

> The word which came to Jeremiah from the LORD, saying: "Arise and go down to the potter's house, and there I will cause you to hear My words." Then I went down to the potter's house, and there he was, making something at the wheel. And the vessel that he made of clay was marred in the hand of the potter; so he made it again into another vessel, as it seemed good to the potter to make. Then the word of the LORD came to me, saying: "O house of Israel, can I not do with you as this potter?" says the LORD. "Look, as the clay is in the potter's hand, so are you in My hand, O house of Israel! The instant I speak concerning a nation and concerning a kingdom, to pluck up, to pull down, and to destroy it, if that nation against whom I have spoken turns from its evil, I will relent of the disaster that I thought to bring upon it. And the instant I speak concerning a nation and concerning a kingdom, to build and to plant it, if it does evil in My sight so that it does not obey My voice, then I will relent concerning the good with which I said I would benefit it. Now therefore, speak to the men of Judah and to the inhabitants of Jerusalem, saying, 'Thus says the LORD: "Behold, I am fashioning a disaster and devising a plan against you. Return now everyone from his evil way, and make your ways and your doings good."'" And they said, "That is hopeless! So we will walk according to our own plans, and we will every one obey the dictates of his evil heart."

Look at these three elements they talked about:

1. The Power of the Potter. Verses 4–6a again: "And the vessel that he made of clay was marred in the hand of the potter; so he made it again into another vessel, as it seemed good to the potter to make. Then the word of the LORD came to me, saying, O house of Israel, can I not do with you as this potter?' says the LORD." Who are we to question God? Isaiah 46:9 says, "Remember the former things of old, for I am God and there is none like Me."

God is sovereign. And we need to recognize the sovereignty of God, the lordship of Jesus Christ. If we're believers, we of all people need to recognize the lordship of Jesus Christ in the sovereignty of God. But whether you're a believer or not, God is sovereign. He is God, and there is no other.

2. The Power of the People. But even in the midst of the power of the Potter, look at the mercy and the grace of God—there is power in the hands of the people. God gives humanity a choice. It's called the free will of people to choose. In verses 7–10, there's some good news, and there's some bad news here. Which would you like first, the good news or the bad news? Well, I'm going to give you the good news first. It's never too late to turn to God. Look at verse 8: "if that nation against whom I have spoken turns from its evil, I will relent of the disaster that I thought to bring upon it." As long as a person, as long as a nation has breath, it is not too late to turn to God. He is merciful. He shows this repeatedly in Scripture. He prefers mercy over judgment. But ultimately, judgment will come if we disobey God.

Now the bad news is this: yesterday's obedience does not secure today's favor of God. Look what he says in verses 9–10: "And the instant I speak concerning a nation and concerning a kingdom, to build and to plant it, if it does evil in My sight so that it does not obey My voice, then I will relent concerning the good with which I said I would benefit it." Now before go on, let me say God has a plan for our nation. I believe God's hand is all over this nation in terms of its founding and its preservation, its protection, its provision. But the same is true for us; if we are disobedient and we repent and turn back to God, He will relent of the curse of the coming judgment. And if we're blessed by God and His favor is upon us, yet we turn from Him, He will relent of that favor and that blessing. Here's the key: It is not about posturing. It's not about proclaiming, "Oh we're a Christian nation. We're a God-fearing people. In God we trust." It's about actually obeying God. The bottom line is obedience, whether it's as a nation or as an individual, as a family. It's not what we hang on our door. It's not what we proclaim in our words. It's what we do in terms of obedience or disobedience to God.

And here's where the clay versus Silly Putty analogy comes in. God makes it abundantly clear that the choice was theirs. He said, "If you turn back to me and obey my voice, I will relent of this destruction that I have proclaimed." And look at how they respond in verse 12: "And they said, 'That is hopeless! So we will walk according to our own plans, and we will every one obey the dictates of his evil heart." They preferred their delusionary idolatry. Rather than yielding to the Potter, they chose to be Silly Putty that reflected the image not of the Creator but of the idols they worshipped. John 3:19 says, "that the light has come into the world, and men loved darkness rather than light, because their deeds were evil." They could not turn to God because they were so wedded to the immorality connected with their idolatry.

3. The Prayer of the Prophet. Now that we've seen the power of the Potter and the power of the people, let's look at the prayer of the prophet. Verse 18: "Then they said, 'Come and let us devise plans against Jeremiah; for the law shall not perish from the priest, nor counsel from the wise, nor the word from the prophet. Come and let us attack him with the tongue, and let us not give heed to any of his words.'" Here's Jeremiah speaking to the Lord in verse 19–20: "'Give heed to me, O Lord, and listen to the voice of those who contend with me! Shall evil be repaid for good? For they have dug a pit for my life. Remember that I stood before You to speak good for them, to turn away Your wrath from them.'" This is the cancel crowd. They're pretending a zeal for the country, for the faith, and declaring the one who spoke truth as the enemy; they wanted to protect the status quo because that was the source of their power. But look at the tactics of the cancel crowd. They blasted his reputation. They wanted to discredit him with the tongue, reject his words, ignore the truth. These are the leaders. These are the ones who were providing the example for the people. They said, "Let's ignore his words, ignore the truth, and then finally, silence him." They wanted to cancel him. They wanted to kill him. So what did Jeremiah do? This is what I want us to focus on. He prayed to the Lord. We just read his prayer. God knows our hearts. This is where we need to go when we face the cancel culture. If you're going to live for God in this environment, you are going to come up against the cancel culture because they have set themselves up as god, as opposed to the one true God. And these idols can be anything we rely upon ahead of God, whether it's our own ability, the wisdom of man.

Let's review how we should respond to the cancel culture? I think the best response is found in Acts 4:29, when the cancel culture crowd came after the disciples for proclaiming the truth of the gospel and threatened them with jail and punishment if they kept preaching and teaching in the name of Jesus. After they were released from the Pharisees and the Sadducees and all the cancel culture crowd of that day, they had a prayer meeting and this is what they prayed: "Now, Lord, look on their threats, and grant to Your servants that with all boldness they may speak Your word." You see, we need to be praying for the boldness to speak the Word of God to a people who would rather be Silly Putty than clay. We need to proclaim the truth of God because Jesus said, "I am the way, the truth, and the life. No one comes to the Father except through Me" (John 14:6). He also said it is the truth that will set you free (see John 8:32). We need to speak truth, so men, women, and children might come to know the true freedom found only in Jesus Christ.

Questions for Reflection and Discussion

1. When God sent Jeremiah to the potter's house to watch him work the clay, what was the message (see vv. 1–11)?
    a. Like the clay in the potter's hand, Israel is in God's hand.
    b. If a nation turns from its evil, God will relent of the judgment He had planned.
    c. If a nation does evil, God will relent of the good He had planned.

d. God is planning judgment for Judah, but He calls on them to repent, offering a way of escape.
e. All of the above.

2. What did the people plot against Jeremiah, and how did he respond (see vv. 18–23)?

Notes on Today's Bible Reading

— DAY 18 —

Today's Reading: Jeremiah 13 and 19

Verse of the Day

> "Behold, I will bring on this city and on all her towns all the doom that I have pronounced against it, because they have stiffened their necks that they might not hear My words."
>
> *Jeremiah 19:15*

Please read the entire Scripture selection in your own Bible and highlight or underline verses that stand out to you before you read the observations and engage the questions below.

When Jeremiah spoke the message of God in Jerusalem in the sixth century before Christ, he spoke to a people who refused to hear the word of God. They were so committed to compromise in the worship of idols that by chapter 19 they had already been consigned to catastrophe. So to a people in that drastic terminal situation, God essentially told Jeremiah, "If they will not hear the message, you must make them see the message." In other words, God instructed Jeremiah to deliver the message to his people by acting it out, performing it. In chapter 13, that message involved burying some underwear, while in chapter 19, it involved smashing a piece of pottery. Unusual actions to communicate God's message visually to a people who refused to hear it verbally.

Let's start with chapter 13. God instructed Jeremiah to go buy some linen underwear, typically like that worn by priests, which would be ordinary for Jeremiah, who was from a priestly lineage. But it would be out of the ordinary to take a long trip in that underwear all the way to the border of Babylon and bury it, an eight-hundred-mile round trip. Can you imagine the conversations about Jeremiah's behavior? Look at verses 4–5: "'Take the sash that you acquired, which is around your waist, and arise, go to the Euphrates, and hide it there in a hole in the rock.' So I went and hid it by the Euphrates, as the LORD commanded me." Time passed, and God told Jeremiah to go back to the Euphrates River and dig up the underwear. When he did, predictably it was rotten and ruined (vv. 6–7). Then came the message: "Thus says the LORD: 'In this manner I will ruin the pride of Judah and the great pride of Jerusalem. This evil people, who refuse to hear My words, who follow the dictates of their hearts, and walk after other gods to serve them and worship them, shall be just like this sash which is profitable for nothing" (vv. 9–10). Idolatry had made God's people as worthless as that rotten, ruined underwear. Yet what Jeremiah did with the underwear was considered odd to communicate the message of God.

Now let's look at chapter 19. God told Jeremiah, "Go and get a potter's earthen flask, and take some of the elders of the people and some of the elders of the priests. And go out to the Valley of the Son of Hinnom, which is by the entry of the Potsherd Gate; and proclaim there the words that I will tell you" (vv. 1–2). According to the Hebrew word, Jeremiah bought an expensive, decorative, earthenware decanter, then he carried it through the streets of the city, which was odd. Women, not men, were seen carrying a pottery jar like that. Somehow Jeremiah convinced a group of civic and religious leaders to follow him and this jar out of Jerusalem to the edge of the valley where they burned their garbage—basically the city dump, which Jesus used as a picture of the perpetual burning of hell (see Mark 9:43 where He refers to *Gehenna*). In verses 10–11, God directed Jeremiah, "Then you shall break the flask in the sight of the men who go with you, and say to them, 'Thus says the LORD of hosts: "Even so I will break this people and this city, as one breaks a potter's vessel, which cannot be made whole again; and they shall bury them in Tophet till there is no place to bury.''" Jeremiah communicated the message of God visually by breaking his pottery jar then verbally delivered the powerful message of God's judgment. In fact, God declared, "Behold, I will bring such a catastrophe on this place, that whoever hears of it, his ears will tingle" (v. 3b).

Not surprisingly, the people viewed Jeremiah's actions as strange and peculiar, eccentric and even bizarre. In the eyes of the witnesses, Jeremiah became odd for the sake of the message of God. He was not alone in the Old Testament. He stood in that brotherhood of the prophets, many of whom performed God's message visually because their people would not listen to the message delivered verbally. Interestingly, Jesus went to the temple, turned over the tables of the merchants and moneychangers, and drove them out. He performed a powerful message. Do you remember how He punctuated it? Jesus quoted Jeremiah when He declared, "It is written, 'My house shall be called a house of prayer,' but you have made it a 'den of thieves'" (see Matt. 21:13; Jer. 7:11).

However, without a doubt, God delivered His greatest message ever when Jesus acted out His death on the cross. The message from this dramatic and drastic action brought different responses. As it was with Jeremiah, some thought what God did through Jesus was odd: "For the message of the cross is foolishness to those who are perishing, but to us who are being saved it is the power of God" (1 Cor. 1:18). Indeed, the cross was God's most powerful message of all. As Paul put it: "But God demonstrates His own love toward us, in that while we were still sinners, Christ died for us" (Rom. 5:8). The original word Paul used translated "demonstrates" means to make something known by action, to show, to put on display. It wasn't enough for God to say He loves us; He showed us He loves us. That is the supreme model for Christ-followers—not to say only the words but to perform the deeds that communicate love. As John put it: "My little children, let us not love in word or in tongue, but in deed and in truth" (1 John 3:18). The question is whether we are willing to risk being considered odd for the sake of faithfully delivering the message of God.

Questions for Reflection and Discussion

1. What did God tell Jeremiah to do with his loincloth (underwear) in chapter 13?
    a. Change it
    b. Wash it
    c. Bury it
    d. Throw it away

2. In chapter 19, what was God's message to the civic and religious leaders from Jeremiah's symbolic action of smashing the pottery flask?

Notes on Today's Bible Reading

— DAY 19 —

Today's Reading: Jeremiah 20

Verse of the Day

> Then I said, "I will not make mention of Him, nor speak anymore in His name." But His word was in my heart like a burning fire shut up in my bones; I was weary of holding it back, and I could not.
>
> *Jeremiah 20:9*

Please read the entire Scripture selection in your own Bible and highlight or underline verses that stand out to you before you read the observations and engage the questions below.

Have you ever become so frustrated in serving the Lord that you wanted to quit? Maybe the only thing that held you back is you just didn't know where to turn in your resignation? This is where we find Jeremiah in chapter 20. Admittedly, it is not that difficult to identify with Jeremiah when you read what happened to him.

Look at verses 1–2: "Now Pashhur the son of Immer, the priest who was also chief governor in the house of the LORD, heard that Jeremiah prophesied these things. Then Pashhur struck Jeremiah the prophet, and put him in the stocks that were in the high gate of Benjamin, which was by the house of the LORD." Apparently, Pashhur was charged with maintaining order in the temple. When he heard about Jeremiah's symbolic action of breaking the flask and his accompanying prophecy, Pashhur took two actions against the prophet. First, he had Jeremiah flogged—forty lashes save one, which is the implication of the Hebrew term used. Second, he had the prophet put in stocks, confined so that his wrists and ankles were secured through a wooden scaffold with his body bent double. So here is Jeremiah, publicly shamed and humiliated and physically beaten and confined simply because he obeyed God, faithfully delivering His message to the people.

The next day, Pashhur released Jeremiah, hoping he had taught the prophet a lesson. But Jeremiah wasn't finished. He declared judgment on Pashhur and the nation of Judah, prophesying that both would be carried away into captivity in Babylon (vv. 3–9). Afterward, the disgraced prophet was upset with God, basically blaming Him for all this trouble, the result of delivering these unpopular messages of judgment in verses 7–8: "O Lord, You induced me, and I was persuaded; You are stronger than I, and have prevailed. I am in derision daily; everyone mocks me. For when I spoke, I cried out; I shouted, 'Violence and plunder!' Because the word of the Lord was made to me a reproach and a derision daily." By this point, Jeremiah wanted to quit, but he could not (v. 9): "Then I said, 'I will not make mention of Him, nor speak anymore in His name.' But His word was in my heart like a burning fire shut up in my bones; I was weary of holding it back, and I could not." What an incredible statement. Jeremiah wanted to stop speaking the message, but God's word burned inside him to the point he was like a volcano that erupted! He was compelled to preach and prophesy God's message!

As he worked through his circumstances, Jeremiah realized that God "had his back": "But the Lord is with me as a mighty, awesome One. Therefore my persecutors will stumble, and will not prevail. They will be greatly ashamed, for they will not prosper. Their everlasting confusion will never be forgotten" (v. 11). In verse 12, Jeremiah asked God to execute vengeance on his persecutors: "But, O Lord of hosts, You who test the righteous, and see the mind and heart, let me see Your vengeance on them; for I have pleaded my cause before You." He broke out in praise in verse 13: "Sing to the Lord! Praise the Lord! For He has delivered the life of the poor from the hand of evildoers." Then in a dramatic shift in emotion, the chapter concludes with

Jeremiah revisiting his shame, even wishing he had not been born (see vv. 14–18).

As we read about what happened to Jeremiah and his state of mind in chapter 20, it is not difficult to sympathize with the prophet. I don't know any believers who would enjoy such shameful and painful treatment. Yet if we are faithful in communicating God's message to our hostile culture, we will be mocked, canceled, even persecuted. Paul makes it plain: "all who desire to live godly in Christ Jesus will suffer persecution" (2 Tim. 3:12). I would not be honest if I said that I never get discouraged, never contemplate quitting when the cancel culture mercilessly mocks and misrepresents what I say. It can be tough to take at times. But Jeremiah 20 contains some encouragement for us when we speak for God, suffer for it, and are tempted to quit: (1) Remember that vengeance belongs to God, so pray for His justice and pray for your persecutors. (2) Remember that stifling the message God has put in your heart just makes for more misery, so proclaim it with courage. (3) Remember that God is with you when you do, so praise Him for His strengthening presence. The Lord stood with Jeremiah as the mighty, awesome One during the prophet's "dark night of the soul" when he wanted to quit. The Lord will stand with you as well. Bear that in mind when you want to quit.

Questions for Reflection and Discussion

1. What happened to Jeremiah as a result of faithfully delivering God's message to the people (see vv. 1–2)?
   a. He was awarded as "Man of the Year."
   b. He was appointed as an elder at the Jerusalem city gates.
   c. He was flogged and thrown in stocks.
   d. None of the above.

2. What did Jeremiah say it was like when he tried not to speak God's message?

Notes on Today's Bible Reading

— DAY 20 —

Today's Reading: Jeremiah 21

Verse of the Day

> "But I will punish you according to the fruit of your doings," says the Lord; "I will kindle a fire in its forest, and it shall devour all things around it."
>
> *Jeremiah 21:14*

Please read the entire Scripture selection in your own Bible and highlight or underline verses that stand out to you before you read the observations and engage the questions below.

I've entitled today's devotion "A Prime Example of Praying for Crop Failure." What do I mean? Well, let's take a look at that in Jeremiah 21, which is the focus for today. When we began the book of Jeremiah, I pointed out that the chapters are not in chronological order. In fact, chapter 21 concerns the final days of the final year of the reign of Zedekiah. Zedekiah was the last king of Judah prior to the destruction of Jerusalem in 586 BC. So with that in mind, let's begin in Jeremiah 21:1–2: "The word which came to Jeremiah from the Lord when King Zedekiah sent to him Pashhur the son of Melchiah, and Zephaniah the son of Maaseiah, the priest, saying, 'Please inquire of the Lord for us, for Nebuchadnezzar king of Babylon makes war against us. Perhaps the Lord will deal with us according to all His wonderful works, that the king may go away from us.'"

Let's put this request of Jeremiah into context. This comes, as I mentioned, near the end of the kingdom. He has been rejected. He's been marginalized. He's been abused. He's been canceled. You name it, he has faced it. What I find interesting here is all of these attacks that came previously to Jeremiah came because he spoke the truth of God, which the people did not want to hear. But look at what occurs when things really get bad. People will ask for help from those whom they know speak the truth, not from those who say what they want to hear. Now this is why, as followers of Jesus Christ, the time in which we are living could lead to one of the greatest harvests of souls in the kingdom of God. We must be faithful to hold fast to the truth of God's Word, proclaiming it first by living it, then as we live it, we need to hold fast to it. Obviously, we cannot do this on our own. In Ephesians 6, when Paul lays out what it means to live the Christian faith, he says, "Finally, my brethren, be strong in the Lord and in the power of His might" (v. 10). We've got to do this in the strength of the Lord. But as we live it then we also speak it, we must remember we will be speaking the truth in the midst of a culture hostile to it. But the reality is, it won't be long until the proverbial "chickens come home to roost," and many, many people are going to be looking for help from those who have been faithful to proclaim truth, even when it was unacceptable.

It's also important to note that the focus of Zedekiah was to ease the symptoms of the people's sin, not to deal with the source, the actual sin that had separated them from the favor and protection of God. Now this stands in sharp contrast to what Hezekiah did about one hundred years previously when the Assyrian king, Sennacherib, laid siege to Jerusalem. Remember, we read that back in 2 Chronicles 32. In that case, Hezekiah humbled himself, and he prayed to God for mercy, along with the prophet Isaiah. And God brought a tremendous deliverance, which is what many believe Zedekiah is referencing when he says in Jeremiah 21:2, "Perhaps the Lord will deal with us according to all His wonderful works, that the king may go away from us." That's what happened previously. Their armies laid siege to Jerusalem, God miraculously intervened, and they went away. The problem is we cannot expect God to do for us what He did for others in the past when we refuse to humble ourselves before Him as they did.

Now let's pick back up in verses 3–6.

> Then Jeremiah said to them, "Thus you shall say to Zedekiah, 'Thus says the LORD God of Israel: "Behold, I will turn back the weapons of war that are in your hands, with which you fight against the king of Babylon and the Chaldeans who besiege you outside the walls; and I will assemble them in the midst of this city. I Myself will fight against you with an outstretched hand and with a strong arm, even in anger and fury and great wrath. I will strike the inhabitants of this city, both man and beast; they shall die of a great pestilence."'"

In this case, God was not going to help them. Instead, He was going to be against them. He set His face against them. This is not a good place to be. In Romans 8:31, Paul writes, "What then shall we say to these things? If God is for us, who can be against us?" On the contrary, what can we say if God *is* against us? I think we can say that we're in big trouble now! Why? Why is God against them here in Jeremiah 21? Well, look at verse 13: "'Behold, I am against you, O inhabitant of the valley, and rock of the plain,' says the LORD, 'Who say, "Who shall come down against us? Or who shall enter our dwellings?"'" They were basically arrogant and proud in their own defenses, thinking they were invulnerable. Well, look what it says in verse 14: "'But I will punish you according to the fruit of your doings,' says the LORD; 'I will kindle a fire in its forest, and it shall devour all things around it.'"

Jerusalem was the center of Jewish life. It was the place of the temple. It was the place for the presence of God. Yet the people had rejected Him and driven out His presence by their choices. And in that vacuum, when we drive out the presence of God, the enemy of our souls will fill it with something that is counter to the truth of God. Notice what He says here in verse 14, "'But I will punish you according to the fruit of your doings,' says the LORD." This reminds me of Proverbs 1:31, which says, "Therefore they shall eat the fruit of their own way, and be filled to the full with their own fancies."

We have discussed this before, but important matters bear repeating. Just as there are physical laws that govern the universe, such as the law of gravity, which are put in place by the Creator, there are moral laws that govern creation as well, whether we acknowledge them or not. Like gravity, it doesn't matter if you acknowledge it or admit it. It's still going to have its effect upon you if you jump off the top of the building. Well breaking God's moral law, sin, has consequences. And let me give a politically incorrect example. Sexual promiscuity has consequences. No one wants to talk about this for fear of being attacked or censored on social media, but the reality is, America is gripped in a pandemic that predates the coronavirus, and it's one that we have absolute control over when we abide by God's moral law, by God's truth. It is a pandemic of sexually transmitted diseases.

In fact, reports say more than 110 million Americans have a sexually transmitted disease with about 20 million new cases each year.[4] Let those numbers sink in. That's nearly one-third of America. That's just one example. But the point is, natural consequences to sin bring about our own demise. Unfortunately, we work to try to ease and eliminate the symptoms, but we refuse to deal with the source. And that's exactly what Zedekiah was doing. They wanted the attack against the city to go away, but they didn't want to deal with the sin, the source of the problem. And that was their rejection of God and His truth. But it got worse for them.

The natural consequences of sin, as I mentioned, bring about our demise because they weaken us, and they make us vulnerable. But then you add to that what we read here, the wrath of God, He says, "I will kindle a fire." Now when God says, "I've set my face against you," that is a bad place to be. But I have no doubt—and this is strictly me, based upon my reading of Scripture and my understanding of the character of God—I believe that had Zedekiah responded like Hezekiah, God would have forgiven Him. Look at Psalm 86:5: "For You, Lord, are good, and ready to forgive, and abundant in mercy to all those who call upon You." You see, I believe that if Zedekiah had responded the way Hezekiah did, who humbled himself before God, He would have stayed His hand of judgment and, in some form or fashion, extended mercy to His people—that's the nature of God.

You see, it's never too late to repent and turn to God. Now that doesn't mean all our problems will go away because there are natural consequences of sin. And here's the deal: God, in His mercy, enables us to deal with those consequences. But the closer we come to that day of reckoning, the harder one's heart becomes, and the less likely repentance will occur. As Paul writes in 2 Corinthians 6:2b, "Behold, now is the accepted time; behold, now is the day of salvation." Don't put off turning back to God.

Questions for Reflection and Discussion

1. With the armies of Babylon advancing, what choice did God give His people (see Jer. 21:9–11)?
   a. Fight or flee
   b. Surrender or die
   c. Neither of the above

2. What measurement did God use in punishing them (see v. 14)?

Notes on Today's Bible Reading

— DAY 21 —

Today's Reading: Jeremiah 22

Verse of the Day

> "Thus says the LORD: 'Execute judgment and righteousness, and deliver the plundered out of the hand of the oppressor.'"
>
> *Jeremiah 22:3a*

Please read the entire Scripture selection in your own Bible and highlight or underline verses that stand out to you before you read the observations and engage the questions below.

The focus in this chapter is on justice. I've entitled this study, "God Requires Justice from Government." What does that mean, especially with all the talk today about social justice? Well, we're going to take a look. In this chapter, Jeremiah delivers a message to the royal family, which is the government. The chapter addresses Jehoahaz, who reigned only three months before he was carried away a captive to Babylon; Jehoiakim, who was king for eleven years; then the final king in this chapter, Jehoiachin, who served for three months. Then there was one more king for eleven years before the destruction of Jerusalem, Zedekiah.

Let's begin in Jeremiah 22:1–5.

> Thus says the LORD: "Go down to the house of the king of Judah, and there speak this word, and say, 'Hear the word of the LORD, O king of Judah, you who sit on the throne of David,

> you and your servants and your people who enter these gates! Thus says the LORD: "Execute judgment and righteousness, and deliver the plundered out of the hand of the oppressor. Do no wrong and do no violence to the stranger, the fatherless, or the widow, nor shed innocent blood in this place. For if you indeed do this thing, then shall enter the gates of this house, riding on horses and in chariots, accompanied by servants and people, kings who sit on the throne of David. But if you will not hear these words, I swear by Myself," says the LORD, "that this house shall become a desolation."'"

Those are some pretty strong words.

It is quiet clear from this message from God through Jeremiah that justice was missing. Now we're not talking about social justice; we're talking about biblically defined justice. And what is that? Look at verse 3a again: "Execute judgment and righteousness, and deliver the plundered out of the hand of the oppressor." That's justice. Making sure people are made whole and do no wrong or violence to the resident alien, the fatherless, or the widow, nor shed innocent blood. In that day, the resident alien, the fatherless, and the widows had no advocates; they were vulnerable, and they were taken advantage of. So it's essentially saying this: "Make sure people are not taken advantage of." And that occurs today as well. The poor are often taken advantage of, those who have no means of access to government. And sometimes we see really the reverse of this in government. That's not justice either! Then there's one other aspect: making sure not to shed innocent blood. We're going to talk more about that in just a moment.

It's clear this message was meant for Jehoiakim, in particular, because by oppression the Levite tribute imposed on Him by Pharaoh Necho from Egypt. He was under tribute to Judah. Consequently, this heavy tribute was placed on them. So he taxed his people. He just passed it on to the people, made them pay the tax, and he took their labor without pay. He made them do public works, in particular building him elaborate palaces, and he didn't pay them. Plus, he shed innocent blood. We talked about that periodically through Jeremiah from a standpoint of the idol Molech, where the people sacrificed their first born to this Canaanite idol. That was one aspect. Manasseh promoted that. But that actually was not the leading issue of the shedding of innocent blood. It was the killing of the prophets. And Jehoiakim participated in that. We'll read about this in chapter 26. Jehoiakim was engaging in religious persecution, and when you have that, when you persecute those who follow the Lord, you cannot have justice. It is the opposite of justice. Our leaders should take note of that today.

Next look at the comparison that God provides between Jehoiakim and Josiah, the last good king, in verses 15–16: "'Shall you reign because you enclose yourself in cedar?'" In other words, he's built these elaborate palaces for himself and has nice homes. And the Lord is asking whether that's what makes him a king? He goes on in the second half of the verse: "'Did not your father eat and drink, and do justice and righteousness? Then it was well with him. He judged the cause of the poor and needy; then it was well. Was not this knowing Me?' says the LORD." To do righteousness and justice is to know the Lord. Or you can reverse that. To know the Lord, you have to do righteousness and justice. Look at verse 17: "'Yet your eyes and your heart are for nothing but your covetousness, for shedding innocent blood, and practicing oppression and violence." Now how did all of this happen? Well we find the answer to that back in verses 8–9. And this is after He warns that desolation is coming upon them if they don't listen to His word and pursue justice. Let's read verse 8: "'And many nations will pass by this city; and everyone will say to his neighbor, "Why has the LORD done so to this great city?"'" Here's the answer. All comes down to this, verse 9: "'Then they will answer, "Because they have forsaken the covenant of the LORD their God, and worshiped other gods and served them."'" What does that have to do with justice, you might ask? Well, where there is no reverence for God, you will be hard pressed to find a respect for man. Proverbs 28:5a says, "Evil men do not understand justice." What is an evil man? A man whose heart is not after the Lord, who does not know the Lord. He cannot understand justice. Why? Psalm 89:14 says, "Righteousness and justice are the foundation of

Your throne; mercy and truth go before Your face." That's what David was saying about the Lord. See evil men do not understand justice, but those who seek the Lord understand all.

Write this down: Fairness and justice are rarely found where there is no fear or reverence of the Creator. It is that fear and reverence that is the foundation for fairness and justice. Yet we have all these cries for "social justice." Well, the reason we're pursuing justice, and justice is missing in our society, is we have removed the foundation, which is a reverence for and a fear of God. He is the foundation. His word and His truth are the foundation for justice. Jesus tells a parable that really sums this up in Luke 18 about an unjust judge who had no fear of God or respect of man. And William Penn, who was the founder of Pennsylvania, sums up the character of government. He says, "Governments, like clocks, go from the motion men give them." And, you know, older folks here know what it means to give a clock a motion. Today we've got these digital watches, but back in the day, you had clocks that you had to wind up and get them moving. The Penn quote continues: "and as governments are made and moved by men, so by them they are ruined too. Wherefore governments rather depend upon men, than men upon governments. Let men be good, and the government cannot be bad; if it be ill, they will cure it."[5] You see, if we want government that will have the blessing and favor of God, it'll be because it dispenses biblically defined justice. If we want the favor of God, that's what we've got to do, rather than have the judgment of God because it facilitates oppression of the people. And if we want that, then we need people in government, men and women in government who know and fear God, which means Christians must be informed and engaged in our government. What does that mean? Certainly, it means voting, but it also means running for office. Some of you should be running for school board or be on the city council, and maybe state legislatures or even Congress.

The bottom line is, God cares about justice, not the sort of woke justice being championed today otherwise known as social justice, but justice as defined by the Word of God. Yet in the absence of biblically defined justice and the foundation of God's Word and His truth, the counterfeit cries for justice get traction, and that only leads to more oppression by the cancel culture.

Questions for Reflection and Discussion

1. What principles of good government did God list as conditions for His blessing (vv. 1–4)?

2. How was King Jehoiakim different from his father Josiah (vv. 15–16)?

Notes on Today's Bible Reading

— DAY 22 —

Today's Reading: Jeremiah 23

Verse of the Day

> "But if they had stood in My counsel, and had caused My people to hear My words, then they would have turned them from their evil way and from the evil of their doings."
>
> *Jeremiah 23:22*

Please read the entire Scripture selection in your own Bible and highlight or underline verses that stand out to you before you read the observations and engage the questions below.

I have entitled this devotion on chapter 23 "A Devastating Combination: Preying Political Leaders and Profane Prophets and Priests." Let's begin in verse 1: "'Woe to the shepherds who destroy and scatter the sheep of My pasture!' says the LORD." Now in this case, when He speaks about the shepherds, He's actually talking about the political leaders. Verse 2: "Therefore thus says the LORD God of Israel against the shepherds who feed My people: 'You have scattered My flock, driven them away, and not attended to them. Behold, I will attend to you for the evil of your doings,' says the LORD." We even talked about this in the previous chapter. How the kings were all about themselves, looking after their own needs and abusing the people—putting heavy taxation upon them and forcing them into labor without compensation.

Let's move on to verses 3–8.

> "But I will gather the remnant of My flock out of all countries where I have driven them, and bring them back to their folds; and they shall be fruitful and increase. I will set up shepherds over them who will feed them; and they shall fear no more, nor be dismayed, nor shall they be lacking," says the LORD. "Behold, the days are coming," says the LORD, "that I will raise to David a Branch of righteousness; a King shall reign and prosper, and execute judgment and righteousness in the earth. In His days Judah will be saved, and Israel will dwell safely; now this is His name by which He will be called: THE LORD OUR RIGHTEOUSNESS. Therefore, behold, the days are coming," says the LORD, "that they shall no longer say, 'As the LORD lives who brought up the children of Israel from the land of Egypt,' but, 'As the LORD lives who brought up and led the descendants of the house of Israel from the north country and from all the countries where I had driven them.' And they shall dwell in their own land."

This is the promise of restoration, after the Babylonian captivity and for a gathering yet to occur fully. And that's from the Diaspora, where those who were scattered, the Jewish people scattered all around the world, would be brought back—a promise yet to be fulfilled. We could say we're seeing that occur to some degree right now, but it's going to come about in totality. And the promise of the Good Shepherd, —Jesus Christ, the Messiah—is that He will reign. He will be the ultimate political leader who will care for the people.

Let's move on to one of the other aspects. It really goes from verse 9 almost through the end of the chapter. It's the profane prophets and priests. Look at verses 11–13: "'For both prophet and priest are profane; yes, in My house I have found their wickedness,' says the LORD. 'Therefore their way shall be to them like slippery ways; in the darkness they shall be driven on and fall in them; for I will bring disaster on them, the year of their punishment,' says the LORD. 'And I have seen folly in the prophets of Samaria: They prophesied by Baal and caused My people Israel to err.'" The prophets, the people who were supposed to speak for God, were speaking for the demonic idols and led the people astray.

There's a reason God describes us as sheep. People are easily led. People need to be led. And that's why leaders are held to a higher account when they preach false words, or they tell people what they want to hear and lead them astray. Verse 14 says, "Also I have seen a horrible thing in the prophets of Jerusalem: They commit adultery and walk in lies; they also strengthen the hands of evildoers, so that no one turns back from his wickedness. All of them are like Sodom to Me, and her inhabitants like Gomorrah." Spiritual compromise leads to moral compromise, and instead of turning them to the Lord and away from their sin, the prophets didn't want to speak the truth because they, too, were dwelling in sin. It strengthened the hands of the evil doers.

You see, this is the result of what this passage describes as profitless preaching, like in verses 16–18.

> Thus says the Lord of hosts: "Do not listen to the words of the prophets who prophesy to you. They make you worthless; they speak a vision of their own heart, not from the mouth of the Lord. They continually say to those who despise Me, 'The Lord has said, "You shall have peace"'; and to everyone who walks according to the dictates of his own heart, they say, 'No evil shall come upon you.'" For who has stood in the counsel of the Lord, and has perceived and heard His word? Who has marked His word and heard it?"

They were telling the people what they wanted to hear. But look what is needed for a profitable ministry, for a ministry that actually brings about a profit in the people, meaning that it brings forth fruit: (1) They should stand. The preachers, the teachers, the pastors—they need to stand in the counsel of the Lord, meaning they need to be people of prayer and people of the Word. (2) They need to preach and proclaim the Word of God, as it says in verse 22: "But if they had stood in My counsel, and had caused My people to hear My Words, then they would have turned them from their evil way and from the evil of their doings." That to me is the key passage in this entire chapter. If they had been in the presence of God, they had been praying, they had been in the Word of God, they had been listening to God—"and had caused My people to hear My words," not their words, not the ideologies and philosophies of man, but the Word of God—"then they would have turned them from their evil way." The pastors, the preachers, the teachers—if they were to proclaim the Word of God, the message they gave would have turned the people from their evil ways and from their evil doings. That's the test of the Word of God. But they didn't do that.

The profane and godless prophets and priests were telling the people what they wanted to hear. Look over in verse 17 where it says, "They continually say to those who despise Me, 'The LORD has said, "You shall have peace"; and to everyone who walks according to the dictates of his own heart, they say, 'No evil shall come upon you.'" So they were telling them what they wanted to hear. Now, that was not isolated to the Old Testament. In his last letter to Timothy before he was executed, Paul wrote, "For the time will come when they will not endure sound doctrine, but according to their own desires, because they have itching ears, they will heap up for themselves teachers; and they will turn their ears away from the truth, and be turned aside to fables" (2 Tim. 4:3–4). You see that's what they were doing. They were telling the people what they wanted to hear. "Oh, don't worry about it; there's going to be peace, and nothing's going to happen. We're going to be good. You can continue as you are." The words they were preaching were their own, and it was what people wanted to hear. It wasn't the Word of God that would convict and bring about repentance if they responded to it. Now, juxtapose this to how the people responded to Jeremiah, who spoke the Word of the Lord. They were actually making a mockery of the Word of the Lord. This is quite a dangerous place to be! And unfortunately, we see it happening in America today where there is an open mockery of the Word of God.

Now let's look at Jeremiah 23:33, "'So when these people or the prophet or the priest ask you, saying, "What is the oracle of the LORD?" you shall then say to them, "What oracle?" I will even forsake you,' says the LORD." They were making light of this. They said, "Oh, what's the burden of the Lord today?" The burden of the Lord was the prophetic message of impending judgment, and they were hearing this so much from Jeremiah, they were just making fun of it. "What's today's news?" "What's today's burden of the Lord?" Now look at verses 34–36: "'And as for the prophet and the priest and the people who say, "The oracle of the LORD!" I will even punish that man and his house. Thus every one of you shall say to his neighbor, and every one to his brother, "What has the LORD answered?" and, "What has the LORD spoken?" And the oracle of the LORD you shall mention no more. For every man's word will be his oracle, for you have perverted the words of the living God, the LORD of hosts, our God.'"

Now here is why the word of the prophets, the pastors, the preachers and teachers must be the Word of God. It is what will transform lives. It is what God has said He will prosper. He has not promised to prosper the Words of pastors and preachers and teachers. He has not promised to prosper the ideologies and philosophies of man. Look at what it says in Isaiah 55:10–11: "'For as the rain comes down, and the snow from heaven, and do not return there, but water the earth, and make it bring forth and bud, that it may give seed to the sower and bread to the eater, so shall My word be that goes forth from My mouth; it shall not return to Me void, but it shall accomplish what I please, and it shall prosper in the thing for which I sent it.'" What is needed now more than ever in the church—everywhere but in our country in particular—are pastors. We need churches led by pastors and preachers who will proclaim the whole council of God, preach the Word of God, unhindered by the cancel culture, unconcerned about political correctness, but will preach and teach the Word of God because that is the only thing that will transform the hearts and minds of people and turn them from their evil ways. It is what convicts all of us. It is what gives us the power to change. And when we do that, we see a society begin to shift because we have that influence. So pray; pray for the teachers, the preachers, the pastors, that they will preach the whole council of God. And quite frankly, if you're in a church where the Word of God is not preached, you need to leave and find a church that is preaching the Word of God. It has the power to change people and transform lives because God has promised His Word will not return to Him void.

Questions for Reflection and Discussion

1. What were the characteristics of the messianic offspring (Branch) of David whom God promised to raise up at a future time (vv. 5–6)?

    a. He will reign as king.
    b. He will deal wisely.
    c. He will execute justice and righteousness.
    d. All of the above.

2. What would have marked the message of the so-called prophets if they had really heard from the Lord (vv. 21–22)?

Notes on Today's Bible Reading

— DAY 23 —

Today's Reading: Jeremiah 24–25

Verse of the Day

> "Thus says the Lord, the God of Israel: 'Like these good figs, so will I acknowledge those who are carried away captive from Judah, whom I have sent out of this place for their own good, into the land of the Chaldeans.'"
>
> *Jeremiah 24:5*

Please read the entire Scripture selection in your own Bible and highlight or underline verses that stand out to you before you read the observations and engage the questions below.

Allow me to remind you again that the chapters in the book of Jeremiah are not always in chronological order. Chapter 24 actually covers a period of time that comes after the setting of chapter 25. Chapter 24 is at the start of the reign of King Zedekiah, which takes place right before captivity begins in earnest for Judah, and it's only ten verses. Let's begin by reading all of them.

> The Lord showed me, and there were two baskets of figs set before the temple of the Lord, after Nebuchadnezzar king of Babylon had carried away captive Jeconiah the son of Jehoiakim, king of Judah, and the princes of Judah with the craftsmen and smiths, from Jerusalem, and had brought them to Babylon. One basket had very good figs, like the figs that are first ripe; and the other basket had very bad figs which

> could not be eaten, they were so bad. Then the LORD said to me, "What do you see, Jeremiah?" And I said, "Figs, the good figs, very good; and the bad, very bad, which cannot be eaten, they are so bad." Again the word of the LORD came to me, saying, "Thus says the LORD, the God of Israel: 'Like these good figs, so will I acknowledge those who are carried away captive from Judah, whom I have sent out of this place for their own good, into the land of the Chaldeans. For I will set My eyes on them for good, and I will bring them back to this land; I will build them and not pull them down, and I will plant them and not pluck them up. Then I will give them a heart to know Me, that I am the LORD; and they shall be My people, and I will be their God, for they shall return to Me with their whole heart. And as the bad figs which cannot be eaten, they are so bad'—surely thus says the LORD—'so will I give up Zedekiah the king of Judah, his princes, the residue of Jerusalem who remain in this land, and those who dwell in the land of Egypt. I will deliver them to trouble into all the kingdoms of the earth, for their harm, to be a reproach and a byword, a taunt and a curse, in all places where I shall drive them. And I will send the sword, the famine, and the pestilence among them, till they are consumed from the land that I gave to them and their fathers.'"

What we have here is God asking Jeremiah to grade the figs. He said there are good figs—they're very good—and there are bad figs—they're very bad. Then God gave the message about both groups of figs. They would be captives because of the sins of the nation, which again we'll see. But look at what God said; He acknowledged the faith of the good figs and extended mercy to them. From what we read, it is likely that the Lord is describing godly people like Daniel and his three friends, Hananiah, Mishael, and Azariah (a.k.a. Shadrach, Meshach, and Abednego), who were carried away in the first Babylonian captivity. These are the good figs. In the midst of a perverse nation and ungodly leadership, there were others who still followed

God or at least attempted to follow the Lord. God promised that He would show them favor in several ways. First, He was going to bring them back to the land. So right here, we see the promise that He's going to bring them back. He was going to build them up. He was going to plant them and establish them, and He was going to place in them a heart that was holy after Him. So, some of these things have not yet been fulfilled, but some have. He brought them (or at least their descendants) back after the Babylonian captivity, but there's still a gathering that's going to take place of the Jewish people, and they will have a heart for God.

Now, what about the bad figs? He's going to deliver them to trouble. God had repeatedly warned them that they were going to reap what they had sown, and they would eat the fruit of their own doings. Remember, what Proverbs 1:31 says, "Therefore they shall eat the fruit of their way, and be filled to the full with their own fancies." He's saying that even though judgment was coming, we see the mercy of God; He was going to set His eyes on them for good. He was going to prosper them. His favor would still be on them in judgment.

We can take encouragement from that as we pray, as we work to see our nation turn back to God. But even if it doesn't, God sees and inspects the fruit. Repeatedly, He says that you will eat the fruit of your own doings. And so we will each stand before God and give an account for what we've done. Of course, as we stand before Him in terms of our eternal salvation, that is only because of the work of the Lord Jesus Christ and placing our trust in Him as our Savior. But even from there, we will give an account of what we do with our lives, whether we serve Him or not. And God, even in the midst of this judgment on the nation, He discerned between the good and the bad; and even to those being carried away, He extended mercy to those that were good fruit, the good figs, and prospered them in what they did.

Now let's quickly look at Jeremiah 25, which goes back to the fourth year of Jehoiakim. Here Jeremiah says he's been basically prophesying the same message for twenty-three years to Judah: "Repent, turn from your evil ways and your evil doings." It's not good enough just to change your mind. You've got to change what you do. That's what he's saying. And in this chapter, he predicts the coming captivity by Nebuchadnezzar and the fact that it's going to last for seventy years.

I just want to point out one thing I found interesting. This is a longer chapter, and I encourage you to read it. We don't have time to cover everything. But one verse that really caught my eye as I was reading through it a number of times was verse 10, which says, "Moreover I will take from them the voice of mirth and the voice of gladness, the voice of the bridegroom and the voice of the bride, the sound of the millstones and the light of the lamp." Now this warning or this curse, however you would describe it, appears four times in the book of Jeremiah, and I just found that as I was looking into it. We see it in two previous chapters, and we'll still see it in chapters to come. But what is interesting is God said in His judgment marriage will decline—it will go away. The prosperity of the home goes away. The security of the home, the light—the lamp that's an oil lamp—would be kept burning all night. That was the security that went away.

It is remarkable to look at the trends today. From the very beginning of my entry into the public arena, I have been working on marriage and family policy, going back twenty-five years. And so I know this data, and I've continued to watch it closely. According to the latest data from the National Center for Health Statistics, marriage rates have hit an all-time low in the United States.[6] We're actually seeing now about 6.5 marriages per 1,000 people. Now that has declined from 2001 when the national rate was 8.2 marriages per 1,000 people. So, it's at an all-time low. Marriage is kind of going away. We're losing the joy that God has designed in that union to create a home. But also, when you look at prosperity, this is very interesting. In a recent research study with the Institute for Family, Wendy Wang indicates that "Millennials who have formed a family by marrying first are significantly less likely to be poor than millennials who have formed a family by having a child before or outside of marriage."[7] Now it goes on to say, "After controlling for education, race, ethnicity, family of origin, income, and a measure of intelligence, knowledge, we find that millennials who married before having any children are about 60% less likely to be poor than their peers who had a child out of wedlock. In fact, 95% of millennials who married first are not poor by the time they are in the late 20s or early 30s." Prosperity, security, marriage—those are things that are being lost in our society. Could that be a part of God judging our nation? And it's not God standing back and passing judgment and simply saying, "You're going to eat the fruit of your own doings." It's something to think about.

I encourage you to read the Bible daily. Visit frc.org/Bible to join our journey through the Bible. As believers, we need to be in the Word of God. It helps us keep everything in perspective of what we're facing. It's so easy to be overcome with anxiety and concern over what is unfolding, but when we begin to see things in the light of Scripture, it gives us perspective. And it offers us hope.

Questions for Reflection and Discussion

1. What was the meaning of the two baskets of figs placed in front of the temple that the Lord showed to Jeremiah (24:4–10)?

2. Compare Jeremiah 25:11 to 2 Chronicles 36:21. How long was Judah's Babylonian captivity to last?

   a. Thirty years
   b. Seventy years
   c. One hundred years
   d. None of the above

Notes on Today's Bible Reading

— DAY 24 —

Today's Reading: Jeremiah 26–27

Verse of the Day

> So the princes and all the people said to the priests and the prophets, "This man does not deserve to die. For he has spoken to us in the name of the Lord our God."
>
> *Jeremiah 26:16*

Please read the entire Scripture selection in your own Bible and highlight or underline verses that stand out to you before you read the observations and engage the questions below.

In today's study, we are going to cover Jeremiah 26–27 and talk about "Overcoming the Cancel Culture." However, I'm going to focus primarily on chapter 26, which comes at the beginning of the reign of King Jehoiakim. Chapter 27 comes during the reign of King Zedekiah when the end is near and God tells them to submit to Nebuchadnezzar. Chapter 27 makes clear that God is the Lord. He uses and directs not only those who acknowledge Him and follow Him but even those who do not recognize Him and those who do not follow him. Why? Because whether we admit it or not, He is the Lord of all. And that's really the message of chapter 27. He says submit, and it'll go well for you, but if you rebel against this chastisement, the judgment that He's bringing through Nebuchadnezzar, then you're going to pay a price. But let's focus on chapter 26, which I believe is as relevant to us today as it was in the time of Jeremiah. Here he's called to stand in front of these hostile and rebellious people and speak the truth of God, knowing the outcome could not only get him canceled but get him killed.

Now we're going to look at the requirement that came from God, the response from the people, the resolve of Jeremiah, and the results. Look at 26:1–2: "In the beginning of the reign of Jehoiakim the son of Josiah, king of Judah, this word came from the LORD, saying, 'Thus says the LORD: "Stand in the court of the LORD's house, and speak to all the cities of Judah, which come to worship in the LORD's house, all the words that I command you to speak to them. Do not diminish a word."'" Now, remember, as we've studied before, while there had been these reforms by Josiah, simultaneously the temple had been restored. People were going back, but their hearts had not fully turned to the Lord. And at the same time, they continued in their idolatry, their immorality. And so Jeremiah's mission continues.

Next look at verse 3: "'Perhaps everyone will listen and turn from his evil way, that I may relent concerning the calamity which I purpose to bring on them because of the evil of their doings.'" Now it says that God would relent. As I say, God will change His mind. He says if we change our ways, the results will be different. God is willing, ready, and able to forgive and to restore; it just depends upon the people. Continuing in verses 4–6: "'And you shall say to them, "Thus says the LORD: 'If you will not listen to Me, to walk in My law which I have set before you, to heed the words of My servants the prophets whom I sent to you, both rising up early and sending them (but you have not heeded), then I will make this house like Shiloh, and will make this city a curse to all the nations of the earth.'"'" What does it mean? We've talked about this before. Make it look like Shiloh. For 369 years, Shiloh was where the tabernacle was located. It was the designated place for the very presence of God. And you remember Eli, the priest who had corrupt sons, and how the Philistines captured the ark of the covenant. That was at the end of Shiloh being the place where God's presence was revealed. So God says here, "I'm going to make it like that—desolate."

1. The Requirement. From God to Jeremiah, the requirement is in verse 2: "Do not diminish a word." I find it very interesting the Lord said, "Look, don't diminish what I'm saying. Don't hold back. I want you to speak the word knowing that it's not going to go over well, knowing that it's going to step on some toes, knowing that people are going to be offended by it. I don't want you to hold back. These are my words, and I want you to speak them." Quite appropriate for us today because it's not our opinion that matters. It really isn't. It's the Word of God. And so we don't need to soften the Word of God and dance around the truth. We need to speak God's truth now. We have to do it from a redemptive heart. And that's what I believe Ephesians 4 says; we're to speak the truth in love, out of a redemptive heart. We're not speaking the Word of God in order to smash somebody or to win a debate. But our goal, our purpose, is to speak truth so that men, women, and children might be free. In John 8:32, Jesus said, "'And you shall know the truth, and the truth shall make you free.'" That's why we speak the truth.

2. The Response. We're going to look at two verses in this next section, Jeremiah 26:8 and 11. Let's start with verse 8: "Now it happened, when Jeremiah had made an end of speaking all that the Lord had commanded him to speak to all the people, that the priests and the prophets and all the people seized him, saying, "You will surely die!" And verse 11: "And the priests and the prophets spoke to the princes and all the people, saying, 'This man deserves to die! For he has prophesied against this city, as you have heard with your ears.'" Now, that sounds exactly like what they tried to do to Jesus over in Matthew 26:59–61, which says, "Now the chief priests, the elders, and all the council sought false testimony against Jesus to put Him to death, but found none. Even though many false witnesses came forward, they found none. But at last two false witnesses came forward and said, 'This fellow said, "I am able to destroy the temple of God and to build it in three days."'" Remember when Jesus said that, and they accused

Him of blasphemy and wanting to tear down the temple, when He was actually talking about His body and the resurrection. But I don't want you to miss the application of what we're looking at here in Jeremiah 26. These religious leaders were not leading people to follow God. They were cultural leaders, as we've previously read, pacifying their fears and telling them what they wanted to hear, following the imaginations of their own heart.

You know, today in America, humanism has become a religion. Now we hear all the time about the separation of church and state and all this kind of stuff. There's a new religion now. They don't have church buildings because they have schoolhouses, and they have government because that is the religion. It's humanism. And we see it in debates such as climate change. We see it in the radical sexual agenda that says you can define your own gender and sex, which is nonsense, totally contrary to science. It's become the new orthodoxy of the Left, and it is a religion. As in Jeremiah's day, when you speak truth and expose a lie, and it *is* a lie, and it's a deceptive lie, you will get pushback. But when you expose a lie and speak the truth, you will face the wrath of the people.

*3. **The Resolve.*** Next notice what Jeremiah does in the face of their response, in verses 12–14: "Then Jeremiah spoke to all the princes and all the people, saying: 'The Lord sent me to prophesy against this house and against this city with all the words that you have heard. Now therefore, amend your ways and your doings, and obey the voice of the Lord your God; then the Lord will relent concerning the doom that He has pronounced against you. As for me, here I am, in your hand; do with me as seems good and proper to you.'" Wow, what a resolve! He said, "Look, I'm just telling you what the Lord told me: You listen to Him, and it's going to go well with you. You don't, and destruction is going to come. But you know what? I trust the Lord and my life is in his hands. You do what you see as right to you." That's courage. That's boldness.

4. The Results. Verse 16: "So the princes and all the people said to the priests and the prophets, 'This man does not deserve to die. For he has spoken to us in the name of the Lord our God.'" Suddenly the priests and the prophets who were leading this charge because they had been exposed to the truth of God had stirred up the people. But Jeremiah had a resolve to stand firm on the truth of God and look what happens. The people began to back away from the priests and the prophets. Look at verses 17–19.

> Then certain of the elders of the land rose up and spoke to all the assembly of the people, saying: "Micah of Moresheth prophesied in the days of Hezekiah king of Judah, and spoke to all the people of Judah, saying, 'Thus says the Lord of hosts: "Zion shall be plowed like a field, Jerusalem shall become heaps of ruins, and the mountain of the temple like the bare hills of the forest."' Did Hezekiah king of Judah and all Judah ever put him to death? Did he not fear the Lord and seek the Lord's favor? And the Lord relented concerning the doom which He had pronounced against them. But we are doing great evil against ourselves."

They go back to history when Hezekiah responded to the Word of the Lord and God spared the city. Now if you read on, you will find there was another prophet that spoke in the name of the Lord, Uriah, and he got scared, and he ran from Jehoiakim and Jehoiakim tracked him down and he killed him. I think there's a lesson here. We cannot be intimidated, and we cannot shrink back. If we show fear in the face of men, we show weakness. And that makes us vulnerable to these attacks. You see, we have to have a resolve knowing that we speak not our own words, but we speak the Words of the Lord.

Now I want to show you one other thing that I think Jeremiah did the entire time that he was facing this cancel culture, and he did it repeatedly. You can go back to the very beginning to when the Lord called him. Look at Jeremiah 1:8, "'Do not be afraid of their faces, for I am with you to deliver you,' says the Lord." And repeatedly He said that He was going to be with him and that he would make him a bronze wall that they could not overcome. And the Lord is with us as we speak His truth. In Matthew 28:20b Jesus says, "'and lo, I am with you always, even to the end of the age.' Amen."

So, I encourage you that just as the disciples in Acts were bold in the face of opposition, we need to be bold as well, because what happens is that intimidates the opponents of the truth. It really kind of turns the table. They want to intimidate us, but as we stand boldly, it intimidates them. And what they plan to do to us happens to them, meaning that they become silent because courage breeds courage. If you stand for God's truth, it won't be long before there are others standing with you.

Questions for Reflection and Discussion

1. When Jeremiah delivered God's message in the temple, what did the priests, prophets, and people say that he deserved (26:1–11)?
   a. The "Prophet of the Year" award
   b. A larger audience
   c. Death
   d. None of the above

2. What visual demonstration did God ask Jeremiah to give and what was the message (27:1–8)?

Notes on Today's Bible Reading

— DAY 25 —

Today's Reading: Jeremiah 28–29

Verse of the Day

> For I know the thoughts that I think toward you, says the Lord, thoughts of peace and not of evil, to give you a future and a hope.
>
> *Jeremiah 29:11*

Please read the entire Scripture selection in your own Bible and highlight or underline verses that stand out to you before you read the observations and engage the questions below.

In chapters 28–29, we have two entirely different scenes. Chapter 28 describes Jeremiah battling, but in chapter 29, Jeremiah communicates God's blessing. Let's begin with chapter 28. A false prophet by the name of Hananiah publicly called out Jeremiah for his "doom and gloom" prophecies about Babylonian control and captivity. See back in chapter 27, when God instructed Jeremiah to once again act out His message to the people by creating bonds and yokes and putting them on. The message from God was to accept the "yoke" of Nebuchadnezzar and the Babylonians. Indeed, Jeremiah declared to King Zedekiah in 27:12b: "'Bring your necks under the yoke of the king of Babylon, and serve him and his people, and live!'" He also warned the king, the leaders, and the people not to listen to these false prophets telling them lies (27:14–18).

Not in the least deterred, the prophet Hananiah contradicted Jeremiah in the temple in the presence of the priests and all the people, or as folk down south put it, "in front of God and everybody." Hananiah fired back and the battle was on. He refuted Jeremiah's message by declaring in 28:2, "'Thus speaks the LORD of hosts, the God of Israel, saying: "I have broken the yoke of the king of Babylon."'" He went on to say that in two years all the sacred items taken from the temple would be returned and Jeconiah, King Jehoiakim's son, and the other captives would return as well (vv. 3–4). Jeremiah returned fire in verses 6–9 and essentially says, "Amen, Hananiah, may the LORD make it so . . . but according to the book of the law, the test of a true prophet is that his prediction come true, otherwise he is to be dismissed as a false prophet" (see Deut. 18:20–22). Battle engaged. Hananiah's response? He broke the yoke off Jeremiah's neck and restated his made-up message about the Lord breaking the yoke of Babylon and bringing back the captives in two years (vv. 10–11). He doubled down. Jeremiah left and went home. Battle over? Not hardly. God sent Jeremiah to Hananiah with two concluding prophetic words: (1) You broke a yoke of wood, but you have put in their place yokes of iron (vv. 13–14). (2) You will die this year "because you have taught rebellion against the LORD" (v. 16). Now the battle is over. Indeed, the last verse of chapter 28 reports: "So Hananiah the prophet died the same year in the seventh month" (v. 17).

What a lesson for those who would presume to speak for God. It is a high and holy calling. It carries enormous responsibility; it means increased scrutiny and heightened accountability to God. No wonder James wrote in his letter, "My brethren, let not many of you become teachers, knowing that we shall receive a stricter judgment" (3:1). So in chapter 28, we see Jeremiah battling with a false prophet, whom the Lord had not sent but had made "this people trust in a lie" (v. 15).

Now in chapter 29, Jeremiah is speaking God's blessing on His people in Babylonian exile by means of a letter to them. No doubt they were discouraged, but God offers them a sense of purpose and hope in verses 5–7: "Build houses and dwell in them; plant gardens and eat their fruit. Take wives and beget sons and daughters; and take wives for your sons and give your daughters to husbands, so that they may bear sons and daughters—that you may be increased there, and not diminished. And seek the peace of the city where I have caused you to be carried away captive, and pray to the LORD for it; for in its peace you will have peace." God gave them a twofold mission: (1) Be fruitful and multiply. (2) Seek the peace, literally the *shalom* or welfare of their new land and pray for it. What would be the result? Two vitally important things: (1) They would increase and not decrease. (2) In the peace of that foreign city, they would enjoy peace themselves.

What an important word *peace* is for Christians in America today! First, be fruitful and multiply. Bloom where you are planted and bear fruit. Increase don't decrease. Second, seek the welfare of your community, your country. We should actively pursue making a positive "salt and light" impact. He added, pray for it. Paul urged in 1 Timothy 2:1–2: "Therefore I exhort first of all that supplications, prayers, intercessions, and giving of thanks be made for all men, for kings and all who are in authority, that we may lead a quiet and peaceable life in all godliness and reverence." It's almost as if Paul was reading Jeremiah 29:7 when he wrote that! Again, the result is so important: For in its *shalom*, you will enjoy peace, well-being too.

After yet another warning about the battle with false prophets (vv. 8–9), God returned to the subject of blessing in verses 10–14.

> For thus says the LORD: After seventy years are completed at Babylon, I will visit you and perform My good word toward you, and cause you to return to this place. For I know the thoughts that I think toward you, says the LORD, thoughts of peace and not of evil, to give you a future and a hope. Then you will call upon Me and go and pray to Me, and I will listen to you. And you will seek Me and find Me, when you search for Me with all your heart. I will be found by you, says the LORD, and I will bring you back from your captivity; I will gather you from all the nations and from all the places where I have driven you, says the LORD, and I will bring you to the place from which I cause you to be carried away captive.

What inspiring words of hope! This declaration would lift the spirits of anyone who is discouraged—especially God's people living in captivity in a pagan land. Perhaps you find yourself discouraged, maybe even a captive of circumstances. Call upon Him. Seek Him. Allow God to breathe fresh hope into your life with His word.

Questions for Reflection and Discussion

1. What symbolic action did the false prophet Hananiah take, and what was God's response through Jeremiah (see 28:10–17)?

2.In his letter to the exiles in Babylon, what did Jeremiah instruct the elders, priests, prophets, and all the people to do (see 29:4–7) ?

   a. Build houses and settle down
   b. Plant gardens and enjoy the produce
   c. Marry and have children
   d. Seek the peace and prosperity of the city in which you live and pray for it
   e. All of the above

Notes on Today's Bible Reading

— DAY 26 —

Today's Reading: Jeremiah 30

Verse of the Day

> The word that came to Jeremiah from the LORD, saying, "Thus speaks the LORD God of Israel, saying: 'Write in a book for yourself all the words that I have spoken to you.'"
>
> *Jeremiah 30:1–2*

Please read the entire Scripture selection in your own Bible and highlight or underline verses that stand out to you before you read the observations and engage the questions below.

In chapter 30, Jeremiah is told to actually write down prophetic words from God into a book. Why a book? So that all of his prophetic messages would be compiled both to serve as encouragement for the exiles, allowing for wider dissemination, and as a word of warning to future generations. As God gave a prophetic word, he carried it out. It speaks to God's sovereignty but also man's responsibility to heed God's warning.

In this chapter, God's message goes beyond the imminent judgment that is coming. It speaks to the future, hope, and promise of restoration not only to the return from Babylon but also to the future day of the Lord, which is yet to come. Now this is just a side note here, but for those who say God is finished with Israel, that runs counter to the Word of God. Many of the promises we read in Jeremiah, and other books of the Old Testament, speak of the future of

Jerusalem, of Israel, and are yet to be fulfilled. And it is during the millennial reign of Christ we'll see these things coming about. Yes, we see obviously some things today that are occurring, a return to the land, but it is not the fulfillment of that prophecy that God speaks of here in Jeremiah.

We're going to look at three aspects of this chapter. I want us to look at the conditions, the calls, and the confidence. And we're read large portions of the chapter here very quickly. As we go through this, I would encourage you to meditate upon it and ask the Holy Spirit to lead you into an understanding of the Word of God. And that's why Jesus said, "I've sent the Holy Spirit." He is the helper. He helps us understand the truth. He said He will lead you into all understanding of the truth. And so we need the Holy Spirit for guidance as we read His Word.

1. The Conditions. Let's start at the beginning.

> The word that came to Jeremiah from the Lord, saying, "Thus speaks the Lord God of Israel, saying: 'Write in a book for yourself all the words that I have spoken to you. For behold, the days are coming,' says the Lord, 'that I will bring back from captivity My people Israel and Judah,' says the Lord. 'And I will cause them to return to the land that I gave to their fathers, and they shall possess it.'" Now these are the words that the Lord spoke concerning Israel and Judah. "For thus says the Lord: 'We have heard a voice of trembling, of fear, and not of peace. Ask now, and see, whether a man is ever in labor with child? So why do I see every man with his hands on his loins like a woman in labor, and all faces turned pale? Alas! For that day is great, so that none is like it; and it is the time of Jacob's trouble, but he shall be saved out of it." (Jeremiah 30:1–7)

So the conditions are: God's judgment is coming upon them.

2. The Cause. What is the cause of this? Again, this is to be written down, so there's clarity as to why the ultimate destruction of Jerusalem took place. Look at verses 13–15: "'There is no one to plead your cause, that you may be bound up; you have no healing medicines. All your lovers have forgotten you; they do not seek you; for I have wounded you with the wound of an enemy, with the chastisement of a cruel one, for the multitude of your iniquities, because your sins have increased. Why do you cry about your affliction? Your sorrow is incurable. Because of the multitude of your iniquities, because your sins have increased, I have done these things to you.'"

Basically, God said, "Don't look to all of those other things you put your trust in, the idols, the culture of the previous inhabitants. They're not going to help you. This is because of your sin. Your pain is incurable. It's because of your guilt and because your sins are just over the top; you just thumbed your nose at God." These are the causes. They brought this judgment on themselves.

3. The Confidence. Now let's look at the third thing, beginning in verse 10: "'Therefore do not fear, O My servant Jacob,' says the Lord, 'Nor be dismayed, O Israel; for behold, I will save you from afar, and your seed from the land of their captivity. Jacob shall return, have rest and be quiet, and no one shall make him afraid.'"

So even as this judgment is coming upon them, the hope is, as God basically said, "I'm going to bring your offspring, not necessarily you." Not many would survive individually the seventy-year captivity they were in, but their offspring would come back. Verse 11: "'For I *am* with you,' says the Lord, 'to save you; though I make a full end of all nations where I have scattered you, yet I will not make a complete end of you. But I will correct you in justice, and will not let you go altogether unpunished.'"

It's very interesting. He says, "You know those nations that I use to judge you? I'm going to judge them." And that's one of the reasons I think it's important we know what God's Word says about Israel. God is not finished with them. He's going to restore them. I want to be on the side of what God is and will do when it comes to His people. Now that doesn't mean we give them a free pass on everything they do. And, you know, Israel is not what Scripture says it will be. It's not there yet. They have not fully returned to God. So when they do things that are contrary to truth, we can't just look the other way. In fact, you know, religious freedom is not something we see abounding in Israel now. It's better than most places in the Middle East, but still, the culture rejects those who turn to Christ.

Let's move on now to verses 16–22.

> "Therefore all those who devour you shall be devoured; and all your adversaries, every one of them, shall go into captivity; those who plunder you shall become plunder, and all who prey upon you I will make a prey. For I will restore health to you and heal you of your wounds," says the LORD, "because they called you an outcast saying: 'This is Zion; no one seeks her.' Thus says the LORD: 'Behold, I will bring back the captivity of Jacob's tents, and have mercy on his dwelling places; the city shall be built upon its own mound, and the palace shall remain according to its own plan. Then out of them shall proceed thanksgiving and the voice of those who make merry; I will multiply them, and they shall not diminish; I will also glorify them, and they shall not be small. Their children also shall be as before, and their congregation shall be established before Me; and I will punish all who oppress them. Their nobles shall be from among them, and their governor shall come from their midst; then I will cause him to draw near, and he shall approach Me; for who is this who pledged his heart to approach Me?' says the LORD. 'You shall be My people, and I will be your God.'"

In the midst of this coming judgment, which is going to be devastating, Jerusalem is about to be under siege by the Babylonians. The temple will finally be destroyed—everything just leveled. The people will be carried away into captivity. But God says, "I'm going to restore you." This was shared among the people in the midst of the captivity in a faraway place absent from everything they had held onto and what gave them a sense of identity.

We see this restoration as the mercy of God. Throughout the book of Jeremiah, we see He gave them the result of their doings. Sin had its consequences, but God's mercy was great. And those principles apply to us today. Yes, we will pay the consequences for the choices we make, but if we turn to God, seeking His forgiveness, turning from our sin, we will find that He is merciful. He is ready and waiting to forgive us of our sins.

I want to close with this passage out of Joel 2:12–14: "'Now, therefore,' says the LORD, 'turn to Me with all your heart, with fasting, with weeping, and with mourning.' So rend your heart, and not your garments; return to the LORD your God, for He is gracious and merciful, slow to anger, and of great kindness; and He relents from doing harm. Who knows if He will turn and relent, and leave a blessing behind Him—a grain offering and a drink offering for the LORD your God?"

Yes, there are consequences for our sins. But God gives us this confidence. This is God's character. He is a God who is forgiving, merciful, and gracious. That's why He sent His son, Jesus Christ. He could have written mankind off because of the multitude of our sins and the repetition of this cycle. But God did not do that. He sent His own son to die for our sins. So by His grace, through faith placed in Him, we will be forgiven of our sins and restored to that relationship with Him. That is our confidence!

Questions for Reflection and Discussion

1. What did God instruct Jeremiah to do with the words that had been revealed to him (see vv. 1–2)?

2. What did God say about the future ruler of His people?
   a. He will be "one of them."
   b. God will make him draw near.
   c. This ruler will approach God when prompted by God.
   d. All of the above.

Notes on Today's Bible Reading

— DAY 27 —

Today's Reading: Jeremiah 31

Verse of the Day

> "Yes, I have loved you with an everlasting love; therefore with lovingkindness I have drawn you."
>
> *Jeremiah 31:3*

Please read the entire Scripture selection in your own Bible and highlight or underline verses that stand out to you before you read the observations and engage the questions below.

In chapter 31, we find the answer to the question, What will last forever? Now this is a continuation of the previous chapter as God spoke to Jeremiah, telling Him to write down these prophecies, which were clearly intended to encourage those who were about to go into captivity, those who would be in captivity, those who would return from captivity—and even us today. The key verse in this chapter is Jeremiah 31:3, which reads in part, "Yes, I have loved you with an everlasting love; therefore with lovingkindness I have drawn you." We're going to look at three aspects in this chapter: (1) God's everlasting love; (2) God's future for His people, Israel; (3) and God's new covenant.

Let's start in Jeremiah 31:1–6.

> "At the same time," says the LORD, "I will be the God of all the families of Israel, and they shall be My people." Thus says the LORD: "The people who survived the sword found grace

> in the wilderness—Israel, when I went to give him rest." The LORD has appeared of old to me, saying: "Yes, I have loved you with an everlasting love; therefore with lovingkindness I have drawn you. Again I will build you, and you shall be rebuilt, O virgin of Israel! You shall again be adorned with your tambourines, and shall go forth in the dances of those who rejoice. You shall yet plant vines on the mountains of Samaria; the planters shall plant and eat them as ordinary food. For there shall be a day when the watchmen will cry on Mount Ephraim, 'Arise, and let us go up to Zion, to the LORD our God.'"

That last verse speaks to a unified Israel, the north and south once again being connected. By the way, the planting of vineyards on the hills of Samaria is occurring today. I don't think it's the ultimate fulfillment of this. This comes in the millennial reign of Christ, but it is happening. We're moving in that direction. In fact, I have planted vines in Samaria.

1. God's Everlasting Love. This first aspect cannot be confused with the idea that God is not also a God of justice and righteousness. We hear about all this. God is love, but God is also justice. God is righteousness. His love does not and cannot cause Him to overlook sin, but rather His love is revealed in His grace through Jesus Christ. We see this in a passage of Scripture we're all familiar with, John 3:16, which says, "For God so loved the world that He gave His only begotten Son, that whoever believes in Him should not perish but have everlasting life." You see, God's love causes Him to pursue us. To use a phrase we're familiar with, God is bending over backward to see people experience His love and not His wrath. Second Peter 3:9 says, "The Lord is not slack concerning His promise, as some count slackness, but is longsuffering toward us, not willing that any should perish but that all should come to repentance." God's love causes Him to pursue us. We read this in Jeremiah 31, where He is like a husband to Israel, pursuing His bride.

2. God's future for His people, Israel. Now let's look at the second aspect of this chapter. If we want to hold claim to God's everlasting love for us, and we can and we should, we must first recognize the promise to Israel. I've said this before, and I'll say it again. Those who want to write off Israel and say they've been replaced by the church are just plain wrong. As we'll see in a moment, biblically we've been grafted in as Gentiles to the covenant, but it is first to Israel. So God loves Israel with an everlasting love. That's why what we see occurring proves there is a future for them. I think the 1948 reestablishment of Israel, Jewish people coming from around the world, is only a precursor. It is not the fulfillment yet of what is to come.

But let's look at Jeremiah 31:31–34.

> "Behold, the days are coming, says the Lord, when I will make a new covenant with the house of Israel and with the house of Judah—not according to the covenant that I made with their fathers in the day that I took them by the hand to lead them out of the land of Egypt, My covenant which they broke, though I was a husband to them, says the Lord. But this is the covenant that I will make with the house of Israel after those days, says the Lord: I will put My law in their minds, and write it on their hearts; and I will be their God, and they shall be My people. No more shall every man teach his neighbor, and every man his brother, saying, 'Know the Lord,' for they all shall know Me, from the least of them to the greatest of them, says the Lord. For I will forgive their iniquity, and their sin I will remember no more."

3. God's New Covenant. This brings us to this chapter's third aspect: the Covenant of Grace, the Gospel Covenant. Paul writes about this in Romans 11. I made reference to this earlier as Gentiles were grafted into this covenant. Now this new covenant promises spiritual blessings whereas the old covenant promised physical blessings. The new is more focused on the internal where the old, the Old Testament, was focused on the external.

The new covenant in Jeremiah 31 has four aspects:

1. God's law will be etched not on tablets but on our minds and hearts. We will have an inward desire to follow God. In this new covenant, the desire and motivation to follow God comes from a love and a desire within, not a fear from without, not external restraints. It's not about ritual. It's not about religion. It's about relationship.
2. We will be the people of God. Our identity is in Christ. It is who we are. We take on that identity of Christ as Paul writes about in the New Testament.
3. There will be a knowledge of God. We won't be reliant upon the priests to speak to God for us, nor the prophets to speak from God to us. We are a royal priesthood. We have the Holy Spirit that leads us into all understanding of the truth. That's what I made reference to earlier. The Holy Spirit is our guide. Jesus said that He would send Him as the comforter and that He would send Him to lead us into all truth. We have the Word of God, and the Holy Spirit is the one who enlightens us and helps us to understand it. So as believers, we have the ability. I know it can sometimes be difficult. We don't understand everything, but as we meditate upon, as we read it, as we pray and ask the Holy Spirit to guide us, we can walk in an understanding of the Word of God and stand upon that Word of God because our identity is found in Christ.
4. Here is the capstone: Jeremiah 31:34, in part, says, "For I will forgive their iniquity, and their sin I will remember no more." We don't have to have a continuous supply of sacrifices to cover our sins. Jesus provided it on the cross. And once we accept His sacrificial death, burial, and resurrection as the atonement for our sin, our sins are removed. As far as the east is from the west, they're gone. We're forgiven. We're free. And we're able to walk in the fullness of life that comes through that relationship with Jesus Christ.

Questions for Reflection and Discussion

1. What would become of the fatalistic proverb, "'The fathers have eaten sour grapes, and the children's teeth are set on edge'" (see vv. 29–30)?

2. What did God say will mark the new covenant with His people?
   a. I will put my law within them, and I will write it on their hearts.
   b. I will be their God, and they shall be my people.
   c. They shall all know me, from the least of them to the greatest.
   d. I will forgive their iniquity, and I will remember their sin no more.
   e. All of the above.

Notes on Today's Bible Reading

— DAY 28 —

Today's Reading: Jeremiah 32

Verse of the Day

> "For thus says the Lord: 'Just as I have brought all this great calamity on this people, so will I bring on them the good that I have promised them.'"
>
> *Jeremiah 32:42*

Please read the entire Scripture selection in your own Bible and highlight or underline verses that stand out to you before you read the observations and engage the questions below.

In chapter 32, we find Jerusalem was in its eleventh hour. Zedekiah was about to enter his eleventh and final year as king of Judah. Nebuchadnezzar was laying siege to Jerusalem. Jeremiah was in prison. Why? Because he had spoken truth to those in power and they didn't like it. Yet even from prison, God led Jeremiah to speak to the impending destruction of the city because of the sins of the people. And also he gave them a word of hope and promise that God was going to do something that looked impossible based upon their present circumstances. He was going to restore the nation to peace and prosperity.

As human beings, generally speaking, I think we have a difficult time looking beyond our present circumstances, especially when we are in times of crises. You know, some, quite frankly, are better than others. And those who are able to envision a future often are set apart from others. While they may be viewed sometimes as odd, they tend to be focused, disciplined, and better able to maintain a positive perspective in the midst of setbacks. And as followers of Jesus Christ, this should describe us. If we understand the long game, or to put it into a more biblically correct term, if we understand the eternal perspective that God has—that we, too, can maintain a sense of peace and stability in times of uncertainty and crisis—we'll tend to be more focused and more disciplined.

Now, let's look at this chapter. It breaks itself into three main parts. The first five verses are introductory. Telling you what I just told you. Then we have a prophetic act—a prayer for understanding, and a promise of a brighter future. So literary events begin in Jeremiah 32:6.

> And Jeremiah said, "The word of the Lord came to me, saying, 'Behold, Hanamel the son of Shallum your uncle will come to you, saying, "Buy my field which is in Anathoth, for the right of redemption is yours to buy it."' Then Hanamel my uncle's son came to me in the court of the prison according to the word of the Lord, and said to me, 'Please buy my field that is in Anathoth, which is in the country of Benjamin; for the right of inheritance is yours, and the redemption yours; buy it for yourself.' Then I knew that this was the word of the Lord. So I bought the field from Hanamel, the son of my uncle who was in Anathoth, and weighed out to him the money—seventeen shekels of silver. And I signed the deed and sealed it, took witnesses, and weighed the money on the scales. So I took the purchase deed, both that which was sealed according to the law and custom, and that which was open; and I gave the purchase deed to Baruch the son of Neriah, son of Mahseiah, in the presence of Hanamel my uncle's son, and in the presence of the witnesses who signed the purchase deed, before all the Jews who sat in the court of the prison. Then I charged Baruch before them, saying, 'Thus says the Lord of hosts, the God of Israel: "Take these deeds, both this purchase deed which is sealed and this deed which is open, and put them in an earthen vessel, that they may last many days."'" (vv. 6–14)

He buys it, does all of the transactions, pays the money, and signs the deeds. He gives it to his cousins and says, "Put this in an earthen vessel that will last a long time." This was a prophetic act. Jeremiah is incarcerated, as I said, for preaching the truth. The nation is about to fall. The temple is going to be destroyed, and the people are going to be carried away into captivity. For a total of seventy years, Jeremiah has prophesied these events. In fact, they are unfolding just as he had said; the siege mounds were outside the city.

Now in the midst of all of this, the Lord tells him, "Redeem a piece of property, family property that is about to be worthless now." Shouldn't Jeremiah be living for today? I mean, many would think, *Why invest money in something that's going to be worthless?* Well, God was saying to Jeremiah, to the people, "You have a future, invest in it." When we often look at the circumstances we're faced with today and we're frantic and where we tend to be drawn into living for today, there's a message here for us: God says, "Live for eternity." Don't lay up things here on this earth where moth and rust destroy, but look into eternity. Look into future generations; invest in them now. To be sure, we may not be the beneficiaries of all the future return on the investment of our time and resources, but others will.

You know, I'm grateful for our leadership in this country. Quite frankly, I didn't agree with everything that Franklin Roosevelt did, but in the 1930s, during the disastrous Dust Bowl years, he led the planting of trees. It didn't reverse the devastation that had already taken place in our nation as a result of the Dust Bowl—not to mention the Depression!—but it provided a more prosperous future for following generations. I benefited from it. I grew up in Oklahoma, where it was kind of the heart of the Dust Bowl. My friend, Dennis Swanberg, talks about planting shade trees that we may never sit under, but our children will. And part of this is having that eternal perspective. It's not all about us. I'm grateful for the Pilgrims who came over four hundred years ago, and they did so not to be the beneficiaries. In fact, half of them died in the first winter. They were not necessarily the beneficiaries; they had quite difficult lives. But as William Bradford wrote in his *Of Plymouth Plantation*, they did it to be simply, if nothing more, steppingstones to the advancement and propagation of the gospel of Jesus Christ.[8] Even if they were just stones that others would step on to take for the truth, they were willing to do it. We've kind of lost that. That's having the long game in mind, having an eternal perspective. To be sure, there is benefit to us in keeping this eternal perspective because we then are not overcome as easily by our present circumstances. It helps us in this as we have this eternal perspective.

Let's look now to the second portion where Jeremiah actually has a prayer for understanding: Jeremiah 32:16–25.

> "Now when I had delivered the purchase deed to Baruch the son of Neriah, I prayed to the Lord, saying: 'Ah, Lord God! Behold, You have made the heavens and the earth by Your great power and outstretched arm. There is nothing too hard for You. You show lovingkindness to thousands, and repay the iniquity of the fathers into the bosom of their children after them—the Great, the Mighty God, whose name is the Lord of hosts. You are great in counsel and mighty in work, for Your eyes are open to all the ways of the sons of men, to give everyone according to his ways and according to the fruit of his doings. You have set signs and wonders in the land of Egypt, to this day, and in Israel and among other men; and You have made Yourself a name, as it is this day. You have brought Your people Israel out of the land of Egypt with signs and wonders, with a strong hand and an outstretched arm, and with great terror; You have given them this land, of which You swore to their fathers to give them—"a land flowing with milk and honey." And they came in and took possession of it, but they have not obeyed Your voice or walked in Your law. They have done nothing of all that You commanded them to do; therefore You have caused all this calamity to come upon them. 'Look, the siege mounds! They have come to the city to take it; and the city has been given into the hand of the Chaldeans who fight against it, because of the sword and famine and pestilence. What You have spoken has happened; there You see

> it! And You have said to me, O Lord God, "Buy the field for money, and take witnesses"!—yet the city has been given into the hand of the Chaldeans.'"

It's interesting what Jeremiah did. He obeyed God. He got the word from the Lord. It was confirmed. His cousin came to this property, and he obeyed. Then he asked for understanding and clarity: "Why, Lord, are you having me to do this?"

Then we see in the third part, there is a promise of a brighter future. Look at verses 26–27: "Then the word of the Lord came to Jeremiah, saying, 'Behold, I am the Lord, the God of all flesh. Is there anything too hard for Me?'" Skip down to verses 37–42.

> "'Behold, I will gather them out of all countries where I have driven them in My anger, in My fury, and in great wrath; I will bring them back to this place, and I will cause them to dwell safely. They shall be My people, and I will be their God; then I will give them one heart and one way, that they may fear Me forever, for the good of them and their children after them. And I will make an everlasting covenant with them, that I will not turn away from doing them good; but I will put My fear in their hearts so that they will not depart from Me. Yes, I will rejoice over them to do them good, and I will assuredly plant them in this land, with all My heart and with all My soul.' For thus says the Lord: 'Just as I have brought all this great calamity on this people, so I will bring on them all the good that I have promised them.'"

You see, God is the merciful God. Yes, He's the God of justice and He's the God of truth, but He is also the God of mercy. And we see this as we have an eternal perspective. Yes, there's difficulty today. We find ourselves in difficulty individually and collectively as a nation, but this is not the end. It helps us if we have an eternal perspective, and there's a couple of ways we can do that. (1) We need to have a relationship with Jesus Christ. He has to be the Lord of our lives, and that means we have to receive forgiveness from Him. We actually see this in this passage where they repented and they came back into relationship with God. We need to be in relationship through this new covenant He actually makes reference to. (2) After we have that relationship, we should spend time in His Word; it will help us understand where we are in perspective of God's view. We have to see ourselves where we are in God's eternal timeline, then it makes a little more sense, and we can find the encouragement we need to continue to be a source of light, a source of encouragement to those around us. So I encourage you to continue to be in the Word of God.

Questions for Reflection and Discussion

1. What did God instruct Jeremiah to do as a symbol of life returning to normal after His people returned from their impending captivity (see vv. 8–15)?

   a. Get married and have children
   b. Buy a field
   c. Learn a new trade
   d. All of the above

2. With Jeremiah witnessing the siege and immanent fall of Jerusalem to the Babylonians, he questioned God's instruction to purchase land. How did God respond to Jeremiah's seeming lack of faith (vv. 26–27)?

Notes on Today's Bible Reading

____

____

____

____

____

____

— DAY 29 —

Today's Reading: Jeremiah 33–34

Verse of the Day

> "In those days and at that time I will cause to grow up to David a Branch of righteousness; he shall execute judgment and righteousness in the earth. In those days Judah will be saved, and Jerusalem will dwell safely. And this is the name by which she will be called: 'The Lord Our Righteousness.'"
>
> *Jeremiah 33:15–16*

Please read the entire Scripture selection in your own Bible and highlight or underline verses that stand out to you before you read the observations and engage the questions below.

We are now in chapters 33–34, and the title of this study is "The Real Discovery Channel." And what do I mean by that? Well, stick with me. I'll get to it at the conclusion. I want to give a quick overview of the two chapters, then I'll focus on something I think is very relevant at the end. It's all relevant, but this in particular encourages me today. And I think you might find it encouraging as well.

In chapter 33, we find Jeremiah is still in prison for preaching the truth. The elite were trying hard to cancel him. They apparently thought that locking him up would shut him up. But notice that the cancel culture of Jeremiah's day could not keep God from speaking as long as Jeremiah was listening. There's a lesson for us now! The Lord again gives the promise of restoration to the nation. And again, this has application to both the return after the Babylonian captivity and the millennial kingdom, which we read about in verses 14–16: "'Behold, the days are coming,' says the LORD, 'that I will perform that good thing which I have promised to the house of Israel and to the house of Judah: "In those days and at that time I will cause to grow up to David, a Branch of righteousness; He shall execute judgment and righteousness in the earth. In those days Judah will be saved, and Jerusalem will dwell safely. And this is the name by which she will be called: THE LORD OUR RIGHTEOUSNESS."'"

We've heard that before, right? And there's only one who can fill that promise: Jesus the Messiah. Also, a side note, the assurance of the fulfillment of the promise of God is creation. Verses 20–21: "'Thus says the LORD: "If you can break My covenant with the day and My covenant with the night, so that there will not be day and night in their season, then My covenant may also be broken with David My servant, so that he shall not have a son to reign on his throne, and with the Levites, the priests, My ministers."'" The point here? We cannot separate God from creation and still understand and know Him. To support this, look over in Romans 1:20–22, "For since the creation of the world His invisible attributes are clearly seen, being understood by the things that are made, even His eternal power and Godhead, so that they are without excuse, because, although they knew God, they did not glorify Him as God, nor were thankful, but became futile in their thoughts, and their foolish hearts were darkened. Professing to be wise, they became fools." We see this passage from Romans playing out in living color today. So God says, "Look, my promise is that I'm going to restore you. And just as the covenant is with the sun and the moon, the day and the night, so this will be fulfilled." God is the Creator, and we have to recognize that we can't truly know God without recognizing Him as the Creator. Even God's attributes are seen in creation itself.

Now in chapter 34, Jeremiah is given a word for King Zedekiah, which is actually a good word, despite the fact that he was a bad king. His life would be spared, and he would be carried to Babylon. It appears in this passage that God gives them one more chance, or at least He tests their hearts one more time. Zedekiah was possibly prompted by the favorable word from Jeremiah. As Paul writes over in Romans 2:4b, "the goodness of God leads you to repentance." Perhaps because God was showing favor to him, he said, "Well, maybe I should turn back to God." So anyway, they make a covenant, and they repent of enslaving their fellow Hebrews. They let them go according to the instructions their fathers had received in Exodus 21. Then apparently what happens is Egypt makes a military move. Babylonian troops withdraw from their siege of Jerusalem to confront the Egyptians, at least temporarily. The people of Judah, thinking the threat has passed, renege on their repentance and enslave their fellow Hebrews again. It's a big mistake, when you commit to God in these emergency conversions, foxhole conversions, but then go back to your old ways. Look at what it says in verse 17: "'Therefore thus says the Lord: "You have not obeyed Me in proclaiming liberty, every one to his brother and every one to his neighbor. Behold, I proclaim liberty to you," says the Lord—"to the sword, to pestilence, and to famine! And I will deliver you to trouble among all the kingdoms of the earth."'"

Here's that one aspect I would like to bring to your attention, which I found encouraging, and I think you will as well. Look back at 33:1–3, "Moreover the word of the Lord came to Jeremiah a second time, while he was still shut up in the court of the prison, saying, 'Thus says the Lord who made it, the Lord who formed it to establish it (the Lord is His name): "Call to Me, and I will answer you, and show you great and mighty things, which you do not know."'" God was making a promise and told Jeremiah and the people to pray for the fulfillment of this promise of restoration. As impossible as it seemed to them at that time, He basically said, "Pray and I will answer you." What we're facing today in our country and our culture may seem impossible for God to bring revival to the church and an awakening to our culture. He says, "Pray and you will discover my faithfulness, and you will see things that you have not known." There it is, the true Discovery Channel.

You and I have the same promises from Jesus. He said this in John 14:12–14: "'Most assuredly, I say to you, he who believes in Me, the works that I do he will do also; and greater *works* than these he will do, because I go to My Father. And whatever you ask in My name, that I will do, that the Father may be glorified in the Son. If you ask anything in My name, I will do it.'" And look what John writes over in 1 John 5:14: "Now this is the confidence that we have in Him, that if we ask anything according to His will, He hears us." That's what God was telling Jeremiah: "Tell the people, look, you don't see this. This is my promise. It doesn't seem possible. Pray, call upon me." Now look at 1 John 5:15: "And if we know that He hears us, whatever we ask, we know that we have the petitions that we have asked of Him." Discover the faithfulness of God's promises, call to Him, and He says He will answer.

Questions for Reflection and Discussion

1. What did God say about the covenant He made with His people (see 33:17–26)?
    a. My covenant is as sure as the fixed laws of nature.
    b. I will make the descendants of David numerous as the stars and sand.
    c. David will never fail to have a descendant on the throne.
    d. All of the above.

2. What did the people do after making a covenant with King Zedekiah to release their slaves (see 34:8–16)?

Notes on Today's Bible Reading

____

____

____

____

____

____

— DAY 30 —

Today's Reading: Jeremiah 35

Verse of the Day

> And Jeremiah said to the house of the Rechabites, "Thus says the LORD of hosts, the God of Israel: 'Because you have obeyed the commandment of Jonadab your father, and kept all his precepts and done according to all that he commanded you, therefore thus says the LORD of hosts, the God of Israel: "Jonadab the son of Rechab shall not lack a man to stand before Me forever."'"
>
> *Jeremiah 35:18–19*

Please read the entire Scripture selection in your own Bible and highlight or underline verses that stand out to you before you read the observations and engage the questions below.

If I were to give chapter 35 a title, it would be "Are You Setting an Example?" Again, we're actually going back in the timeline from previous chapters here in chapter 35. We've been studying chapters concerning the end, when Zedekiah was king right before the final destruction of Jerusalem. Here we go back to a period between 609 BC and 598 BC, when Jehoiakim was king. Remember, he reigned for eleven years. Now this episode occurs on one of the occasions when Nebuchadnezzar is about to invade Jerusalem. We know that it occurred on two occasions, first in 605 BC after he defeated the Egyptian army and he made Israel a vassal state, putting Jehoiakim under his reign but then Jehoiakim rebelled. Then in 598 BC, Nebuchadnezzar came back and took away captives, which likely included

Daniel and his three friends. The final destruction didn't come until about ten years later. So in chapter 35, God instructs Jeremiah to use a faithful family as an example to an unfaithful nation. I want you to pay close attention because this is fascinating. I'm going to include a large portion of this relatively short chapter.

Let's begin by reading Jeremiah 35:1–11.

> The word which came to Jeremiah from the Lord in the days of Jehoiakim the son of Josiah, king of Judah, saying, "Go to the house of the Rechabites, speak to them, and bring them into the house of the Lord, into one of the chambers, and give them wine to drink." Then I took Jaazaniah the son of Jeremiah, the son of Habazziniah, his brothers and all his sons, and the whole house of the Rechabites, and I brought them into the house of the Lord, into the chamber of the sons of Hanan the son of Igdaliah, a man of God, which was by the chamber of the princes, above the chamber of Maaseiah the son of Shallum, the keeper of the door. Then I set before the sons of the house of the Rechabites bowls full of wine, and cups; and I said to them, "Drink wine." But they said, "We will drink no wine, for Jonadab the son of Rechab, our father, commanded us, saying, 'You shall drink no wine, you nor your sons, forever. You shall not build a house, sow seed, plant a vineyard, nor have any of these; but all your days you shall dwell in tents, that you may live many days in the land where you are sojourners.' Thus we have obeyed the voice of Jonadab the son of Rechab, our father, in all that he charged us, to drink no wine all our days, we, our wives, our sons, or our daughters, nor to build ourselves houses to dwell in; nor do we have vineyard, field, or seed. But we have dwelt in tents, and have obeyed and done according to all that Jonadab our father commanded us. But it came to pass, when Nebuchadnezzar king of Babylon came up into the land, that we said, 'Come, let us go to Jerusalem for fear of the army of the Chaldeans and for fear of the army of the Syrians.' So we dwell at Jerusalem."

The first point I want us to see here is the influence of a father. Matthew Henry points out that this family line was originally the Canaanites, and they appear in 1 Chronicles 2:55.

> These are the Kenites who came from Hammath, the father of the house of Rechab. And the Kenites, at least those of them that gained settlement in the land of Israel, were the posterity of Hobab, the father-in-law of Moses, who we read about in Judges 1:16. Now we find him separated from the Amalekites and one of these families the Kenites had their denomination from Rechab. His son or lineage descended from him was Jonadab, a man famous in his time for wisdom and piety. He flourished in the days of Jehu, king of Israel, nearly 300 years before that.[9]

So this father who set this example had lived three hundred years before this occurrence where Jeremiah brings them into the temple, sets them in this place of influence, and places wine before them and they refuse to drink it.

There were two commands or instructions Jonadab gave. One is regarding temperance, exercising self-control. They refused to drink the wine. And they were living in Jerusalem now where wine was everywhere. In fact, at one point we see it was a problem. There was too much wine. Discipline is a good thing. So that was, in part, why Jonadab left this instruction of self-control. It's a good thing for us and our families to have discipline, to instruct our children and challenge them to live a disciplined and strict life.

Second, temporal is the other focus, exercising a proper understanding of this world. They lived in tents. Not being focused on this world, quite frankly, made them a hardy bunch. They lived on the land they had. They were shepherds. They didn't plant. They didn't sit in one place. They were in tents, and they moved around. They were subjected to more of the elements. It kept their focus in the right way. Now there was no commandment to do this from God, but what Jonadab did was set an example, and no doubt he lived this way. But there was wisdom in what he instructed, and he encouraged his children and those who came after him to do so.

Let's pick back up with Jeremiah 35:12–15.

> Then came the word of the Lord to Jeremiah, saying, "Thus says the Lord of hosts, the God of Israel: 'Go and tell the men of Judah and the inhabitants of Jerusalem, "Will you not receive instruction to obey My words?" says the Lord. "The words of Jonadab the son of Rechab, which he commanded his sons, not to drink wine, are performed; for to this day they drink none, and obey their father's commandment. But although I have spoken to you, rising early and speaking, you did not obey Me. I have also sent to you all My servants the prophets, rising up early and sending them, saying, 'Turn now everyone from his evil way, amend your doings, and do not go after other gods to serve them; then you will dwell in the land which I have given you and your fathers.' But you have not inclined your ear, nor obeyed Me."'"

So here we see the example of a faithful family. Jeremiah pulled them in and set this wine before them. He didn't first ask them if they wanted wine. He set bowls filled with wine and cups, ready to dip in, even in the trappings of the temple. Somehow they didn't take the bait. They were not tempted. They were resolute in their living. So as a result, they're used as an example to an unfaithful nation; you see, they resisted the pressure to conform.

We see in verse 11 where they dwelled in Jerusalem because of Chaldean and Syrian armies coming in. So they came there for safety. Now they were to live in tents. But obviously these were instructions for an emergency; there was grace from a standpoint that they didn't live under the bondage of this. They used it as guidance and direction. So they come into the city, yet they refused to conform to the city. They lived *in* the city, but they didn't live *like* the city. And I think that's an example to us today as families in a culture that seems to have given way to everything that happens in the world. And this occurs in the church as well. It's sometimes hard to distinguish between a Christian family and a non-Christian family. We're so influenced by the culture. Yet we see from the Rechabites that they were able to live in a city but not live like the city. And they were held up as an example of faithfulness to an unfaithful nation.

I think today can be the same, when we, as followers of Jesus Christ, live according to the Lord's direction for our lives. He can hold us up as an example, which I believe attracts others—when we live according to the instructions of God, life is a little smoother. It doesn't mean we don't have challenges, but it means that we have a sense of peace; we have a sense of mission and purpose. And quite frankly, that's what most people are looking for in this world.

Let's continue in verses 18–19: "And Jeremiah said to the house of the Rechabites, 'Thus says the LORD of hosts, the God of Israel: "Because you have obeyed the commandment of Jonadab your father, and kept all his precepts and done according to all that he commanded you, therefore thus says the LORD of hosts, the God of Israel: 'Jonadab the son of Rechab shall not lack a man to stand before Me forever.'"'" That is the legacy of faithfulness here. God said to the nation of Judah that if they just simply obeyed Him and followed His guidance, they could dwell in the land forever. Here we see a faithful family, who even in the impending destruction, he said, "Look, you will never fail to have a man standing before Me because of your obedience and faithfulness." God honors faithfulness.

I end this day's study with a story I ran across a number of years ago. It is the comparison of two men from the 1700s, who both lived in New York. The first was Max Jukes. "Jukes did not believe in Christ, nor did he give his children Christian training. He refused to take his children to church even when they asked. He has had over 1026 descendants, 300 of whom were sent to prison for an average term of thirteen years. Some 190 were prostitutes and 680 were admitted alcoholics. His family members cost the state hundreds of thousands of dollars, and they made no known contribution to society. The other man was Jonathan Edwards. He loved the Lord and saw that his children were in church every Sunday. He served the Lord to the best of his ability. Of his 929 descendants, 430 were ministers, 86 became university professors, 13 became university presidents, 75 wrote positive books, 7 were elected to the U.S. Congress, and one served as vice president of the United States. His family never cost the state one cent, but contributed immeasurably to the common good."[10] That's an example of godly living. As fathers, as families, we can be an example to the world around us. So the question is, are you setting an example? And if so, what kind?

Questions for Reflection and Discussion

1. How did Jeremiah test the Rechabites?
   a. Put a plate of pork in front of them
   b. Put bowls of wine before them
   c. Both of the above
   d. Neither of the above

2. What lesson did the Lord teach the men of Judah and Jerusalem through the lives of the Rechabites, and what reward did they receive as a result of their obedience (35:12–19)?

Notes on Today's Bible Reading

— DAY 31 —

Today's Reading: Jeremiah 36

Verse of the Day

> And it happened, when Jehudi had read three or four columns, that the king cut it with the scribe's knife and cast it into the fire that was on the hearth, until all the scroll was consumed in the fire that was on the hearth.
>
> *Jeremiah 36:23*

Please read the entire Scripture selection in your own Bible and highlight or underline verses that stand out to you before you read the observations and engage the questions below.

The question for today's study is this: "Can God's Word be canceled?" Let's find out. In chapter 36, we see a stark contrast. We read about King Josiah and his response to the reading of God's rediscovered Word. Godly Josiah tore his clothes in repentance, wept over their sin and rebellion, and humbly asked for a word from the Lord (see 2 Kings 22; 2 Chronicles 34). Yet we see the diametrically opposite reaction from his son, King Jehoiakim, who brazenly burned the prophecies of Jeremiah, which are also God's Word.

Jeremiah carefully wrote down everything God told him in the hope "that the house of Judah will hear all the adversities which I purpose to bring upon them, that everyone may turn from his evil way, that I may forgive their iniquity and their sin" (v. 3). But Jeremiah could not deliver this message at the temple because verse 5 says he was banned from going to the house of the Lord. Can you imagine? Oh wait, we just came out of the pandemic where we saw the same thing, didn't we? So he sent his scribe Baruch, who read the scroll at the temple, and the Word of God went over like a skunk at a wedding. It caused no small stir among the royal officials. Consequently, Baruch was immediately pulled aside by some of the princes and officials who ultimately told Baruch and Jeremiah to go into hiding. The government men then stored the scroll.

The officials reported the gist of the prophet's message, but King Jehoiakim was not satisfied. He didn't want a summary or even a paraphrase, he wanted that scroll of what is now Scripture. According to verse 22, it was the ninth month (December); the king was sitting in the winter house, and a fire burned in the fire pot before him. Look at verses 23–26.

> And it happened, when Jehudi had read three or four columns, that the king cut it with the scribe's knife and cast it into the fire that was on the hearth, until all the scroll was consumed in the fire that was on the hearth. Yet they were not afraid, nor did they tear their garments, the king nor any of his servants who heard all these words. Nevertheless Elnathan, Delaiah, and Gemariah implored the king not to burn the scroll; but he would not listen to them. And the king commanded Jerahmeel the king's son, Seraiah the son of Azriel, and Shelemiah the son of Abdeel, to seize Baruch the scribe and Jeremiah the prophet, but the Lord hid them.

Can you picture this? Jehudi reads a little, and the king cuts it off and tosses it in the flames. He reads a little more, and the king cuts it off and tosses it in the flames. And this process goes on until the ruler has burned about thirty chapters or so of the book. Unbelievable! And not only that, but verse 24 says there was no response from the king or his servants. Contrast their response with that of good King Josiah, who humbly repented and wept at the reading of God's Word. However, there were some God-fearing officials present who begged the king not to do such an outrageous thing as burn what we know now is God's Word. They probably thought lightning was about to strike any moment and didn't want to be collateral damage from God's judgment! But this ruler was so blatantly brash in his rebellion against God and His word that he didn't care. Can you imagine anyone who would have the audacity to try to cancel God's Word by brazenly burning it as it is being read?

Let me give you a recent example, which occurred in the U.S. Congress. While no one burned the Bible, God's Word was nonetheless canceled as irrelevant. In debating against the so-called Equality Act in the House Chamber, Rep. Greg Steube (R-FL) read from God's Word in Deuteronomy 22:5 regarding what we call today transgenderism. However, Rep. Jerry Nadler (D-NY) responded, "Mr. Steube, what any religious tradition ascribes as God's will is no concern of this Congress."[11] Unbelievable. The audacity of that man, standing in front of the motto "In God We Trust"and with his back to the only full-face relief among twenty-three renowned lawgivers and that House Chamber—a portrait of Moses, who delivered God's law and is the basis of *our* law—the very law quoted by Rep. Steube. To say that God's will expressed in His Word is of no concern of this Congress was breathtakingly brazen. It flies in the face of more than 230 years of our heritage as a constitutional republic. While not as dramatic as burning part of the Bible, as King Jehoiakim did, it is nevertheless shocking. Yet how many times do we, after having heard the Word of God faithfully preached or having read it ourselves, casually ignore what it says, effectively acting in the same way. This is a convicting word for our nation and for us all.

As for the prophet Jeremiah and Baruch his scribe, God hid them. They were protected from the wrath of the king, but Jeremiah was not done. According to verse 32, Jeremiah took another scroll and gave it to Baruch and dictated all of it again, plus even more! The result is the book of Jeremiah. Just as Isaiah said, "'The grass withers, the flower fades, but the word of our God stands forever'" (40:8). The point is, you cannot cancel God's Word, no matter how much one disagrees with it or dislikes it. The word of God will stand forever. The questions we all need to ask are, Do we hear it (or read it) and ignore it, or do we reverently obey it?

Questions for Reflection and Discussion

1. When God told Jeremiah to write down on a scroll all the words He had spoken to him since the days of King Josiah, instructed his assistant Baruch to read it in the temple, and it was ultimately taken and read to King Jehoiakim, what did the king ultimately do with the scroll (see 36:22–24)?

   a. Placed the scroll in the royal library
   b. Repented in sackcloth and ashes
   c. Cut it in strips and tossed it in the fire
   d. None of the above

2. After the king burned the scroll, what did God instruct Jeremiah to do?

Notes on Today's Bible Reading

— DAY 32 —

Today's Reading: Jeremiah 37–38

Verse of the Day

> But Jeremiah said, "They shall not deliver you. Please, obey the voice of the LORD which I speak to you. So it shall be well with you, and your soul shall live."
>
> *Jeremiah 38:20*

Please read the entire Scripture selection in your own Bible and highlight or underline verses that stand out to you before you read the observations and engage the questions below.

Today we are studying chapters 37 and 38, events that occurred chronologically before chapter 32 (Jeremiah was not yet in prison; see 37:4). In chapter 37, Nebuchadnezzar had deposed Coniah (Jehoiachin) and put his twenty-one-year-old uncle Mattaniah (meaning "Gift of Yahweh") on the throne. In fact, Nebuchadnezzar renamed him "Zedekiah," meaning "Yahweh is my righteousness," which is ironic because he is evaluated as having done "evil in the sight of the LORD" (see 52:2). Like most puppet rulers, he was weak and vacillating. Zedekiah was a small man in a big moment with the fate of the nation on the line. In taking the throne, Zedekiah pledged loyalty to Nebuchadnezzar. However, pro-Egypt sentiment among the royal leadership prevailed, and Zedekiah ultimately decided to rebel, which brought the full weight of Nebuchadnezzar's wrath against Judah, ultimately resulting in the final siege and destruction of Jerusalem. This could have been avoided had Zedekiah listened to the Lord. Yet 37:2 tells us, "But neither he nor his servants nor the people of the land gave heed to the words of the LORD which He spoke by the prophet Jeremiah."

Although Zedekiah didn't listen to Jeremiah, the king nevertheless wanted Jeremiah's prayers in a crisis (see 37:3): "And Zedekiah the king sent Jehucal the son of Shelemiah, and Zephaniah the son of Maaseiah, the priest, to the prophet Jeremiah, saying, 'Pray now to the LORD our God for us.'" When Zedekiah asked for prayer, the Babylonian army threatened Jerusalem. Have you noticed that when people get desperate they want prayer? It seems to be their last resort, not their first response.

When the Babylonians left Jerusalem and went south to meet the Egyptian army, it seemed to King Zedekiah a dramatic answer to prayer, indeed a miracle from heaven. The Babylonian siege was temporarily broken, and Jerusalem seemed to have been rescued by the Egyptians. Yet that event inspired not only more false hope but more rejection of Jeremiah's message that they needed to capitulate to Babylon or be crushed and carried away into captivity. Jeremiah tried to convince them (vv. 5–10). However, his prophetic word from the Lord was not simply ignored, it was considered treasonous.

In fact, Jeremiah was treated as a traitor, hauled in before the princes, who had Jeremiah beaten and thrown into a dungeon (see vv. 11–15). However, Zedekiah secretly summoned Jeremiah from prison (v. 17): "then Zedekiah the king sent and took him out. The king asked him secretly in his house, and said, 'Is there any word from the LORD?' And Jeremiah said, 'There is.' Then he said, 'You shall be delivered into the hand of the king of Babylon!'" Prison didn't make Jeremiah change his tune. He came out singing yet another verse! Indeed, Jeremiah boldly asked Zedekiah where all his false prophets were, who had predicted wrongly about Nebuchadnezzar invading Judah. However, he was languishing in that dungeon to the point he believed he would die if he was taken back, so he asked the king for mercy. To his credit, Zedekiah complied and had Jeremiah placed in the court of the prison and given a daily food ration (see vv. 18–21).

Just when it looked like his circumstances had improved, things go downhill for Jeremiah in chapter 38. Again, the message Jeremiah had been preaching was considered seditious and treasonous by the cancel crowd. So the princes were fed up with him and took their case to King Zedekiah in verse 4: "'Please, let this man be put to death, for thus he weakens the hands of the men of war who remain in this city, and the hands of all the people, by speaking such words to them. For this man does not seek the welfare of this people, but their harm.'" Being the weak king that he was, Zedekiah didn't even put up a fight for the only man who told him the truth and really the best friend he had: "'Look, he is in your hand. For the king can do nothing against you'" (v. 5). Talk about a fair-weather friend; that was Zedekiah. Look at verse 6: "So they took Jeremiah and cast him into the dungeon of Malchiah the king's son, which was in the court of the prison, and they let Jeremiah down with ropes. And in the dungeon there was no water, but mire. So Jeremiah sank in the mire." Can you imagine?

Yet in this dire situation, up to his armpits in mud, Jeremiah found that he indeed had a true friend in the palace (vv. 7–9): "Now Ebed-Melech the Ethiopian, one of the eunuchs, who was in the king's house, heard that they had put Jeremiah in the dungeon. When the king was sitting at the Gate of Benjamin, Ebed-Melech went out of the king's house and spoke to the king, saying: 'My lord the king, these men have done evil in all that they have done to Jeremiah the prophet, whom they have cast into the dungeon, and he is likely to die from hunger in the place where he is. For there is no more bread in the city.'"

The name Ebed-Melech means servant of the king. He was an Ethiopian, not a Jew. Perhaps he had immigrated to Judah or had been taken prisoner and turned into a servant to the king. But here's what is significant about Ebed-Melech: He feared God more than man. He trusted God, and he acted in obedience to God out of fear and reverence for God and for the man of God—and God rewarded him. And by the way, it's interesting, a God-fearing Ethiopian eunuch was among the first converts to Christ as a result of Philip's mission in Acts (see 8:26–39), and many Ethiopians continue to be strong believers to this day.

Of course, we read on that the king, who seemed to be easily swayed by everyone except Jeremiah, acquiesced in verse 10: "'Take from here thirty men with you, and lift Jeremiah the prophet out of the dungeon before he dies." So, Ebed-Melech executed a daring and determined effort to rescue Jeremiah from the miry pit and took care of him, literally saving his life (vv. 11–13). The second half of the chapter (vv. 14–28) features King Zedekiah asking Jeremiah for yet another secret meeting to get a word from the Lord, which Jeremiah faithfully gives. The message had not changed, so Jeremiah was sent back to prison where he remained until Jerusalem fell to the Babylonians—but at least he wasn't stuck in that pit.

What are the lessons we can learn? First, obedience to God often comes at the price of rejection and even persecution. But second, God has people, sometimes unlikely people, in strategic places, whom He will send at just the right moment to come alongside to help us. Then third, we must persevere in prayer, then with eyes of faith, see what God is doing through His servants sent to assist us. Don't lose hope in that pit. Pray for God to send help. In His time, He will. So keep praying and watching for that person. Indeed, if all human help fails, the true Ebed-Melech, Jesus Himself, is coming. Help is on the way!

Questions for Reflection and Discussion

1. After Jeremiah was beaten and imprisoned, King Zedekiah brought the prophet out of prison to secretly ask if there was any word from the Lord for him. After delivering that word, what did Jeremiah ask of the king (see 37:16–21)?
   a. Spare him from the dungeon
   b. Provide him daily food
   c. Compensate him for spiritual counsel
   d. All of the above

2. When they became fed up with Jeremiah's message of judgment during the Babylonian siege of Jerusalem, what did some of the leading men do to the faithful prophet (see 38:1–6)?

Notes on Today's Bible Reading

— DAY 33 —

Today's Reading: Jeremiah 39–40

Verse of the Day

> "'For I will surely deliver you, and you shall not fall by the sword; but your life shall be as a prize to you, because you have put your trust in Me,' says the LORD."
>
> *Jeremiah 39:18*

Please read the entire Scripture selection in your own Bible and highlight or underline verses that stand out to you before you read the observations and engage the questions below.

Today we are looking at chapters 39–40. We're going to talk about the results when you trust the Lord. However, the first verses of chapter 39 give us the sad account of the fall of Jerusalem. The Babylonian army breached the walls, poured into the city, overthrew it, and captured the palace and burned it to the ground. Then according to chapter 52, they burned the temple down. They also found King Zedekiah, took him captive, put out his eyes, and led him away to Babylon. Later in chapters 40–45, we have the account of what happened in the nation after the destruction of Jerusalem. Now you would think that the destruction of Jerusalem and the temple would be enough to turn the hearts of the people back to God but not so. These people had not reached the bottom yet.

Our focus, however, is on the latter part of chapter 39. And the central verse for our study today is Jeremiah 39:18, which says, ""'For I will surely deliver you, and you shall not fall by the sword; but your life shall be as a prize to you, because you have put your trust in Me," says the LORD.'" Jeremiah had been warning Judah for forty years that they needed to mend their ways and their doings and obey the law, so the Lord might relent of the coming judgment that He had pronounced upon Judah. Now an interesting parallel is in the New Testament with the ministry of Jesus, who some said was Jeremiah. Jeremiah didn't say that judgment might come. He said that judgment was coming unless they repented. And Jesus said something similar in John 3:17–18: "For God did not send His Son into the world to condemn the world, but that the world through Him might be saved. He who believes in Him is not condemned; but he who does not believe is condemned already, because he has not believed in the name of the only begotten Son of God." So just as Judah did in Jeremiah's day, we stand condemned. But when we turn to the Lord and, by faith, accept Jesus Christ as our Lord and Savior from the grace of God, we are saved. Then our lives are transformed by God's truth, and our ways and our doings are amended.

Another aspect I want to focus on today is the same instrument, Nebuchadnezzar, delivered both God's wrath and His mercy. What was the determining factor? That's what we'll look at through Jeremiah 39:11–18.

> Now Nebuchadnezzar king of Babylon gave charge concerning Jeremiah to Nebuzaradan the captain of the guard, saying, "Take him and look after him, and do him no harm; but do to him just as he says to you." So Nebuzaradan the captain of the guard sent Nebushasban, Rabsaris, Nergal-Sharezer, Rabmag, and all the king of Babylon's chief officers; then they sent someone to take Jeremiah from the court of the prison, and committed him to Gedaliah the son of Ahikam, the son of Shaphan, that he should take him home. So he dwelt among the people. Meanwhile the word of the LORD had come to Jeremiah while he was shut up in the court of the prison, saying, "Go and speak to Ebed-Melech the Ethiopian, saying, 'Thus says the LORD of hosts,

> the God of Israel: "Behold, I will bring My words upon this city for adversity and not for good, and they shall be performed in that day before you. But I will deliver you in that day," says the LORD, "and you shall not be given into the hand of the men of whom you are afraid. For I will surely deliver you, and you shall not fall by the sword; but your life shall be as a prize to you, because you have put your trust in Me," says the LORD.'"

Now I want to look quickly at two things. First, God had promised Jeremiah He was going to deliver him, and He made good on that promise. We go back to the very beginnings of Jeremiah's call in chapter 1 where He says, "'Do not be afraid of their faces, for I am with you to deliver you,' says the LORD." So here's the promise to the prophet: "If you trust me, I'll take care of you." And so he repeatedly told Jeremiah, "Look, I'm going to deliver you. You will be spared." Jeremiah had a difficult job facing the opposition—being thrown in prison three times, one time in a dungeon, a miry pit to where death was the only way out—but the Lord spared him. Then we read here in this chapter that Nebuchadnezzar had Jeremiah set free from prison (39:11–14).

Second, that brings us to this Ethiopian Ebed-Melech, whom we met in the previous chapters, the one who delivered Jeremiah out of that pit. Ebed-Melech showed mercy to Jeremiah. So God told Jeremiah in verses 15–18 that He would show mercy to Ebed-Melech and deliver him. Why? Because God said in verse 18: "'you have put your trust in Me,' says the LORD." In Galatians 6:7, Paul says, "Do not be deceived, God is not mocked; for whatever a man sows, that he will also reap." See when we trust God, God is faithful. Remember, Ebed-Melech was a servant of the king, not a Jew, but he had a fear of God. In fact, he had a greater reverence for God than he had a fear of man. So, as he trusted God, he acted to deliver Jeremiah out of that pit. You see, trust in God should result in actions for God. You can't trust God and do nothing. You must trust and obey. And as you obey, God will take care of you. That happened for Ebed-Melech.

So the very instrument that God used to bring judgment and punishment upon Judah was the same instrument that brought mercy to Jeremiah and Ebed-Melech. When we see distressing events around us today, we don't have to be concerned about the circumstances and be fretful and anxious about what tomorrow may bring or what may happen. The same circumstances that bring others into a very dire, desperate situation, and even the punishment of God, will be the same circumstances that, as we walk in obedience to God, trusting Him and obeying Him, can bring about His mercy to us. Consequently, don't put your eyes on the world and the circumstances around you. Put your eyes on the Lord. And regardless of what is happening in the world today, obey Him and follow His Word. If we trust Him, He will prove Himself faithful to us, just as He has throughout the history of humankind.

Questions for Reflection and Discussion

1. What happened to the prophet Jeremiah when the Babylonians took over the city of Jerusalem (39:11–14)?

2. When given the choice, what did Jeremiah decide to do (see 40:1–6)?
   a. Go with the captives into Babylon
   b. Stay with the survivors in Judah
   c. Neither of the above

Notes on Today's Bible Reading

— DAY 34 —

Today's Reading: Jeremiah 41–42

Verse of the Day

> Then Jeremiah the prophet said to them, "I have heard. Indeed, I will pray to the LORD your God according to your words, and it shall be, that whatever the LORD answers you, I will declare it to you. I will keep nothing back from you."
>
> *Jeremiah 42:4*

Please read the entire Scripture selection in your own Bible and highlight or underline verses that stand out to you before you read the observations and engage the questions below.

I've titled this study "God Doesn't Have a Rubber Stamp." In chapters 41–42, we see the trouble in Judah continues even after the final destruction of Jerusalem. Gedaliah had been set up as a puppet governor over the remnant Nebuchadnezzar left, but there was a coup attempt by Ishmael, a member of the royal family. In fact, Ishmael succeeds in murdering Gedaliah then shamelessly murders a host of loyal worshippers of God in chapter 41. However, Ishmael is then confronted by Johanan and the captains of the remaining forces, and the rebel flees. That brings us to chapter 42, where those who remain under the leadership of Johanan approach Jeremiah for direction. And we'll see they really didn't want direction. They wanted affirmation of what they had already determined to do. That's the "rubber stamp" I'm talking about.

Let's dive into chapter 42, beginning in verses 1–6.

> Now all the captains of the forces, Johanan the son of Kareah, Jezaniah the son of Hoshaiah, and all the people, from the least to the greatest, came near and said to Jeremiah the prophet, "Please, let our petition be acceptable to you, and pray for us to the LORD your God, for all this remnant (since we are left but a few of many, as you can see), that the LORD your God may show us the way in which we should walk and the thing we should do." Then Jeremiah the prophet said to them, "I have heard. Indeed, I will pray to the LORD your God according to your words, and it shall be, that whatever the LORD answers you, I will declare it to you. I will keep nothing back from you." So they said to Jeremiah, "Let the LORD be a true and faithful witness between us, if we do not do according to everything which the LORD your God sends us by you. Whether it is pleasing or displeasing, we will obey the voice of the LORD our God to whom we send you, that it may be well with us when we obey the voice of the LORD our God."

That sounds pretty good. So there's three aspects I want us to look at: (1) the request of the people, (2) the response of the prophet, and (3) the results of the petition.

1. The Request of the People. The people say, "Pray for us that we will have God's direction." Now that is a good thing, and we need to be praying for God's direction as well. But here is how Jesus taught His disciples to pray over in Luke 11:2: "So He said to them, 'When you pray, say: Our Father in heaven, hallowed be Your name. Your kingdom come. Your will be done on earth as it is in heaven.'" The key is God's will, not our way. We need to be praying it is God's will that be accomplished in our lives, not going to Him and asking Him to affirm what we've decided to do or to rubber stamp what we want done. Over in 1 John 5:14–15, he speaks to the power of praying according to the will of God: "Now this is the confidence that we have in Him, that if we ask anything according to His will, He hears us. And if we know that He hears us, whatever we ask, we know that we have the petitions that we have asked of Him." So it appears that Johanan and those there were approaching this in the right way. But we need to be clear that, when we're praying to God, we're asking for God's direction; it's not only in our words but in our heart that we are seeking the will of God.

2. The Response of the Prophet. Now let's look at Jeremiah's response, which is telling and gives us direction. Look again at Jeremiah 42:4: "Then Jeremiah the prophet said to them, 'I have heard. Indeed, I will pray to the LORD your God according to your words, and it shall be, that whatever the LORD answers you, I will declare it to you. I will keep nothing back from you.'" This should be the posture of those who proclaim the Word of God. It's not our opinions that matter. And as much as we may detest and want to avoid conflict or even hurting people's feelings as pastors, teachers, preachers, and followers of Christ, we must be true to our calling. And that is, we declare the whole council of God; we must preach the Word of God, be ready in season and out of season, convince, rebuke, and exhort—with all long in teaching.

So the response of Jeremiah is, "I will pray." And we should always be willing to pray even for those who have strayed, those who may be opposed to us. We should always be willing to pray for those who want prayer. But here's the key: we have to pray according to the will of God, and we have to declare the Word of God. In those days, the prophet spoke from God to the people. Of course, they didn't have the priests. They had been carried away. So they went to the prophet asking them to intercede with God on their behalf. But as those who proclaim the Word of God, we have to proclaim the whole council of God. We cannot hold anything back. We have to speak truth, even in the face of this cancel culture. The truth is, in this age of moral relativism, rejected. But we still are bound to proclaim the truth of God if we're going to speak as instruments and messengers of God.

3. The Result of the Petition. Their intentions now are exposed. It takes ten days. Jeremiah goes and he prays for ten days and he comes back with an answer. But their intentions were clear. Verse 20 says,

"For you were hypocrites in your hearts when you sent me to the LORD your God, saying, 'Pray for us to the LORD our God, and according to all that the LORD your God says, so declare to us and we will do it.'" He knew God showed him their hearts were not before Him. They wanted a Word from God that would put a rubber stamp of approval on their plans, and their plans were being shaped by their fear and not their faith. Look again at verses 11–12: "'Do not be afraid of the king of Babylon, of whom you are afraid; do not be afraid of him,' says the LORD, 'for I am with you, to save you and deliver you from his hand. And I will show you mercy, that he may have mercy on you and cause you to return to your own land.'" God promised them what they were searching for if they would simply obey Him.

Now it's not enough to seek the Lord. We must also follow and obey Him. They went to the Lord in prayer. They asked for direction. But of course their hearts were exposed. They were wanting God to rubber stamp what they had already planned to do. But God said, "Look, I know your plans have been shaped by fear, fear of Nebuchadnezzar because of what happened with Ishmael killing Gedaliah." And they were fearful. I mean, they had just witnessed this devastation. God said, "Look, I will protect you." And so rather than letting their plans dictate their steps, which were shaped by their fear of man, God said, "Have faith in me and allow me to direct your steps."

It's interesting because this is the same issue that Jeremiah brought before the people of Judah over and over again. And he said, "Amend your ways and your doings." It's not just enough to go to God. You have to obey God as well. But God makes it clear what happens if they choose to do it their way. Look what it says in verses 15–16: "'Then hear now the word of the LORD, O remnant of Judah! Thus says the LORD of hosts, the God of Israel: "If you wholly set your faces to enter Egypt, and go to dwell there, then it shall be that the sword which you feared shall overtake you there in the land of Egypt; the famine of which you were afraid shall follow close after you there in Egypt; and there you shall die."'" The very thing they were afraid of, the very fears directing and guiding their steps and shaping their plans, were going to come upon them. This is what Proverbs 10:24 states: "The fear of the wicked will come upon him, and the desire of the righteous will be granted." Do not let your fears determine your plans. Let God determine your plans as you truly seek Him in faith and obey Him.

Questions for Reflection and Discussion

1. What happened to Gedaliah, the Babylonian's puppet ruler over the survivors in Judah in chapter 41?

2. What word from the Lord did Jeremiah deliver to the leaders of Judah in chapter 42?
    a. If you stay in the land, then I will bless you and deliver you from the king of Babylon.
    b. If you go down to Egypt, then I will curse you with the sword, famine, and pestilence.
    c. All of the above.

Notes on Today's Bible Reading

— DAY 35 —

Today's Reading: Jeremiah 43–44

Verse of the Day

> "As for the word that you have spoken to us in the name of the LORD, we will not listen to you!"
>
> *Jeremiah 44:16*

Please read the entire Scripture selection in your own Bible and highlight or underline verses that stand out to you before you read the observations and engage the questions below.

Today we're in Jeremiah 43–44, and I've titled this study "When Sin Becomes Sacred." Our key verse is in chapter 44, but in chapter 43, the remaining leadership takes everyone down to Egypt—all the remnant, those left behind when Nebuchadnezzar carried everybody else off to Babylon, and this includes Jeremiah. In both chapters 43 and 44, we have the first and final message from God to those who went to Egypt. It is a message they had heard many times from Jeremiah during his forty years of ministry and prophecy: repent and turn from your idolatry. But what we see in chapter 44 is almost without parallel, and it's open and determined defiance of God.

Let's begin in 44:1–4.

> The word that came to Jeremiah concerning all the Jews who dwell in the land of Egypt, who dwell at Migdol, at Tahpanhes, at Noph, and in the country of Pathros, saying, "Thus says the LORD of hosts, the God of Israel: 'You have seen all the

> calamity that I have brought on Jerusalem and on all the cities of Judah; and behold, this day they are a desolation, and no one dwells in them, because of their wickedness which they have committed to provoke Me to anger, in that they went to burn incense and to serve other gods whom they did not know, they nor you nor your fathers. However I have sent to you all My servants the prophets, rising early and sending them, saying, 'Oh, do not do this abominable thing that I hate!'"

Now consider for a moment where these people are. They had left the destruction of Judah and Jerusalem and fled to Egypt thinking they would be beyond the reach of Babylon. And of course, in the previous chapter, the Lord gave the prophetic message they were going to be tracked down there in Egypt and they were going to suffer the same consequences because they disobeyed God. But here, not only do they have the Word of God warning them about the effects of idolatry; they saw it. They saw the destruction of Judah, yet they refused to turn back to God.

Let's continue in verses 5–7: "'But they did not listen or incline their ear to turn from their wickedness, to burn no incense to other gods. So My fury and My anger were poured out and kindled in the cities of Judah and in the streets of Jerusalem; and they are wasted and desolate, as it is this day.' Now therefore, thus says the Lord, the God of hosts, the God of Israel: 'Why do you commit this great evil against yourselves, to cut off from you man and woman, child and infant, out of Judah, leaving none to remain . . .'"

You see, our sin is not only against God, but it negatively affects us. I mean, our defiance against God ultimately leads to our own destruction. In other words, if we were smart and we wanted what was best even for ourselves, we would follow and obey God. Now continue in verse 8–11.

> "'. . . in that you provoke Me to wrath with the works of your hands, burning incense to other gods in the land of Egypt where you have gone to dwell, that you may cut yourselves

> off and be a curse and a reproach among all the nations of the earth? Have you forgotten the wickedness of your fathers, the wickedness of the kings of Judah, the wickedness of their wives, your own wickedness, and the wickedness of your wives, which they committed in the land of Judah and in the streets of Jerusalem? They have not been humbled, to this day, nor have they feared; they have not walked in My law or in My statutes that I set before you and your fathers.' Therefore thus says the LORD of hosts, the God of Israel: 'Behold, I will set My face against you for catastrophe and for cutting off all Judah.'"

That's a bad place to be when God says, "I'm setting my face against you for harm." Now look at verse 12: "'And I will take the remnant of Judah who have set their faces to go into the land of Egypt to dwell there, and they shall all be consumed and fall in the land of Egypt. They shall be consumed by the sword and by famine. They shall die, from the least to the greatest, by the sword and by famine; and they shall be an oath, an astonishment, a curse and a reproach!'" This is the very things they were trying to escape in Judah—the sword and famine. And they thought, *Well, we're going to run to Egypt, and we'll find protection there rather than obeying God and trusting Him.*

However, as we read in Jeremiah 44:13–18,

> "For I will punish those who dwell in the land of Egypt, as I have punished Jerusalem, by the sword, by famine, and by pestilence, so that none of the remnant of Judah who have gone into the land of Egypt to dwell there shall escape or survive, lest they return to the land of Judah, to which they desire to return and dwell. For none shall return except those who escape." Then all the men who knew that their wives had burned incense to other gods, with all the women who stood by, a great multitude, and all the people who dwelt in the land of Egypt, in Pathros, answered Jeremiah, saying: "As for the word that you have spoken to us in the name of the LORD, we

> will not listen to you! But we will certainly do whatever has gone out of our own mouth, to burn incense to the queen of heaven and pour out drink offerings to her, as we have done, we and our fathers, our kings and our princes, in the cities of Judah and in the streets of Jerusalem. For then we had plenty of food, were well-off, and saw no trouble. But since we stopped burning incense to the queen of heaven and pouring out drink offerings to her, we have lacked everything and have been consumed by the sword and by famine."

This goes back to the reforms of Josiah when he began to take down the high places and remove the worship of either the moon or the sun god or the host of heaven. There's some debate as to which deity or if it was all of the celestial hosts they were worshipping when it comes to the moon, the stars, and the sun. But the point is, they were worshipping the creation, not the Creator.

Now how does sin become sacred? I think we find the answers here in these last three verses: (1) They suppressed the Word and the truth of God. (2) They ceased being thankful to God, attributing His blessings to the creation of their own hands. Oftentimes we read that God in His grace and mercy, trying to woo his people back, will bless them and prosper them. And oftentimes, this outpouring of God's grace is mistaken as a favor from sin. They attributed His blessings to the worship of idols. They said, "Look, we were doing fine when we were worshipping the hosts of heaven, when we were worshipping the queen of heaven." And (3) they elevated the creation over the Creator.

This pattern is clearly outlined in Romans 1, a chapter people don't like to read. They don't want to hear it because it is a clear delineation of the pattern that leads to sin becoming sacred. Look at Romans 1:18–25.

> For the wrath of God is revealed from heaven against all ungodliness and unrighteousness of men, who suppress the truth in unrighteousness, because what may be known of God is manifest in them, for God has shown it to them. For since

> the creation of the world His invisible attributes are clearly seen, being understood by the things that are made, even His eternal power and Godhead, so that they are without excuse, because, although they knew God, they did not glorify Him as God, nor were thankful, but became futile in their thoughts, and their foolish hearts were darkened. Professing to be wise, they became fools, and changed the glory of the incorruptible God into an image made like corruptible man—and birds and four-footed animals and creeping things. Therefore God also gave them up to uncleanness, in the lusts of their hearts, to dishonor their bodies among themselves, who exchanged the truth of God for the lie, and worshiped and served the creature rather than the Creator, who is blessed forever. Amen.

It is evident they had completed this devolvement because they attributed the chastisement of God, designed to bring them to repentance, as the effects of neglecting their sin. In other words, the sacred had become sin and sin had become sacred.

Look at Jeremiah's response in Jeremiah 44:23–27.

> "Because you have burned incense and because you have sinned against the Lord and have not obeyed the voice of the Lord or walked in His law, in His statutes or in His testimonies, therefore this calamity has happened to you, as at this day." Moreover, Jeremiah said to all the people and to all the women, "Hear the word of the Lord, all Judah who are in the land of Egypt! Thus says the Lord of hosts, the God of Israel, saying: 'You and your wives have spoken with your mouths and fulfilled with your hands, saying, "We will surely keep our vows that we have made, to burn incense to the queen of heaven and pour out drink offerings to her." You will surely keep your vows and perform your vows!' Therefore, hear the word of the Lord, all Judah who dwell in the land of Egypt: 'Behold, I have sworn by My great name,' says the Lord, 'that My name shall no more be named in the mouth of any man of

> Judah in all the land of Egypt, saying, "The Lord GOD lives." Behold, I will watch over them for adversity and not for good. And all the men of Judah who are in the land of Egypt shall be consumed by the sword and by famine, until there is an end to them.'"

They were going to keep their vows, and God was vowed that He would not relent from the destruction because of their disobedience.

I must be quite candid here. This should have alarm bells ringing in America. Our country is following the same path—where the sacred, serving the Lord Jesus Christ in every aspect of our lives, in our homes, in our workplaces, and in our schools, has become sin in the eyes of the political and cultural elites. And what God has clearly called sin has become sacred or celebrated and protected by government and the prevailing culture. Commenting on this chapter, Matthew Henry wrote this: "Daring sinners may speak many a bold word and many a big word, but after all, God will have the last word."[12] Big tech and the cultural elites might cancel God's prophets, but they cannot cancel God. He will have the final word.

Questions for Reflection and Discussion

1. What reaction did the arrogant men of Judah have to the word of the Lord through Jeremiah (see 43:2–4)?

2. How did the people of Judah who had fled to Egypt respond to the word of the Lord Jeremiah delivered to them (see 44:16–19)?
   a. Dug in their heels and refused to repent
   b. Voiced their commitment to idols
   c. Credited their prosperity to the "queen of heaven"
   d. All of the above

Notes on Today's Bible Reading

— DAY 36 —

Today's Reading: Jeremiah 45–47

Verse of the Day

> "And do you seek great things for yourself? Do not seek them; for behold, I will bring adversity on all flesh," says the LORD. "But I will give your life to you as a prize in all places, wherever you go."
>
> *Jeremiah 45:5*

Please read the entire Scripture selection in your own Bible and highlight or underline verses that stand out to you before you read the observations and engage the questions below.

Our reading covers Jeremiah 45–47. In chapters 46–47, we enter a new portion of Jeremiah's prophecy to the nations surrounding them. Remember, when God called him as a teenager, He told the young man: "'See, I have this day set you over the nations and over the kingdoms, to root out and to pull down, to destroy and to throw down, to build and to plant'" (1:10). Consequently, in chapters 46–51, we see Jeremiah sending God's messages of judgment to the various nations around Judah, beginning with messages to Egypt in chapter 46 and to Philistia in chapter 47—with a promise to preserve Israel sandwiched in between (see 46:27–28). We will explore more on these messages to the nations in the next study.

Today's focus, however, will be on chapter 45. The title of the study is "Finding the Prize in Life." Remember the prizes they used to put in

Cracker Jacks or cereal boxes? As a child, I remember the little prizes, little toys would be nearly at the bottom of the box. Great motivation to eat a second bowl of cereal and a tremendous marketing strategy. But those prizes actually had value in those days. We didn't have a lot of toys, and so a rubber ball in the cereal box really had some value to it. As we look at this chapter, we will see that God told a disheartened, discouraged, and disillusioned servant that He had a prize for him. What was that prize? Well, let's take a look at it.

Chapter 45 represents quite a short message that went to Jeremiah's servant, or scribe, Baruch. This chapter takes us back almost twenty years previous, to the fourth year of the reign of Jehoiakim. The chapter could have been inserted after chapter 36 when these events took place. This was when Baruch wrote down the words of Jeremiah onto a scroll. Jeremiah had been what would be the equivalent of de-platformed of the day. He was banned from going to the town square where people communicated, and that was at the temple. He couldn't go because the equivalent of Big Tech of that day had canceled him. So Jeremiah called Baruch, wrote down the words on the scroll, and he sent Baruch to the temple to read the words that the Lord had given Jeremiah. This message was consistent with the previous messages that God had delivered through Jeremiah. The bottom line? Repent! The nation was to repent, turn from their ideology, idolatry, and their sin, or face the fury of the Lord. But the response to the message was such that Baruch was driven from public and forced into hiding. It was apparently not the career path Baruch had planned for himself.

Here is Jeremiah 45.

> The word that Jeremiah the prophet spoke to Baruch the son of Neriah, when he had written these words in a book at the instruction of Jeremiah, in the fourth year of Jehoiakim the son of Josiah, king of Judah, saying, "Thus says the LORD, the God of Israel, to you, O Baruch: 'You said, "Woe is me now! For the LORD has added grief to my sorrow. I fainted in my sighing, and I find no rest." Thus you shall say to him, 'Thus

> says the Lord: "Behold, what I have built I will break down, and what I have planted I will pluck up, that is, this whole land. And do you seek great things for yourself? Do not seek them; for behold, I will bring adversity on all flesh," says the Lord. "But I will give your life to you as a prize in all places, wherever you go."'"

We can assume Baruch was an educated, talented young man, a scholar. He had a future. It is quite possible when he joined Jeremiah, the man of God, that Baruch assumed this post would include an honorable position. Jeremiah was called by God, and I'm certain he had hopes and expectations the nation would respond to that Word of repentance and Jeremiah would be elevated to an honorable position, like Isaiah before him. So consider the blow to this young man when he had to go into hiding after delivering the message. The king went after him, and he sought him, not to reward him but to exact revenge.

No not only did Baruch, like Jeremiah, have to bear a burdensome message of God's impending judgment, but on top of that, he had to face personal rejection. That was the cancel culture. This reminds me of what Jesus told His disciples, which includes all of those who follow Him, including us today. In John 15:20, He said, "Remember the word that I said to you, 'A servant is not greater than his master.' If they persecuted Me, they will also persecute you. If they kept My word, they will keep yours also." Also, Baruch and Jeremiah are a similar parallel between us and Jesus. Remember, I've said this before, but when Jesus asked, "Who do the men say that I am?" some thought He was Jeremiah, the weeping prophet. And so, as a servant of Jesus, just as Baruch was a servant of Jeremiah, we carry the same message. It's not our message. It's the message of the Lord. And if they rejected what God had to say through Jesus, they're going to reject us too. And then there'll be some, as Jesus said, that will receive what you have to say, because some received what He had to say. But we must face this reality of following Jesus.

Here's what one scholar had to say regarding this passage in Jeremiah 45. He said, "The frowns of this world would not disquiet us as they do if we did not foolishly flatter ourselves with the hopes of its smiles in court and covet them too much. It is our overfondness for the good things of this present time that makes us impatient under its evil things."[13] So what are we to do now? I mean, we all want to be accepted. We want the affirmation of those around us. But if our eyes are upon the world, and we're delivering a message that is inconsistent with what the world thinks, we can't expect the world to applauded us. So, what are we to do? Well, Paul provides the answer over in Colossians 3:2. He says, "Set your mind on things above, not on things on the earth." You see, this earth is not our home and the world is not who we should be living for. Our eyes should be on Jesus, the Author and the Finisher of our faith. And here is the promise found in 1 John 2:17, which is similar to the promise that God gave Baruch: "And the world is passing away, and the lust of it; but he who does the will of God abides forever." See if we'll do the will of God, even as all of this world is passing away, we will find the prize of life.

Questions for Reflection and Discussion

1. What message did the Lord give to Jeremiah's scribe, Baruch, when he felt the burden of serving God through serving the prophet and pitied himself (45:4–5)?

   a. What I have built, I am breaking down; what I have planted, I am plucking up.
   b. Do not seek great things for yourself, for I am bringing disaster on all flesh.
   c. Wherever you go, I will spare your life as a prize of war.
   d. None of the above.

2. What words of comfort did Jeremiah have for God's people even as He pronounced judgment on the surrounding nations in these chapters (see 46:27–28)?

Notes on Today's Bible Reading

— DAY 37 —

Today's Reading: Jeremiah 48

Verse of the Day

> "Moab shall be ashamed of Chemosh, as the house of Israel was ashamed of Bethel, their confidence."
>
> *Jeremiah 48:13*

Please read the entire Scripture selection in your own Bible and highlight or underline verses that stand out to you before you read the observations and engage the questions below.

As I pointed out briefly in our last study, Jeremiah 46–51 are prophecies God gave Jeremiah against the surrounding nations. Jeremiah begins with Egypt in chapter 46, which is where he was living at the time he compiled this section of messages, and he ends far to the east in the land of Babylon, across the Euphrates River. But today, we focus briefly on chapter 48, which is a word of judgment leveled specifically at Moab, one of Israel's ancient enemies. I also want to look at a few of the underlying truths and messages we find in chapters 46–51, which are prophecies of judgment upon the nations surrounding Judah and Israel. Most of these prophecies came years before the destruction of Jerusalem, which took place in 586 BC.

So first, I want us to see that God punished Israel and Judah for their idolatry, their pride, and their wickedness. Then He systematically judged the other nations for their pride, idolatry, and wickedness. It reminds me of what 1 Peter 4:17–18 says: "For the time has come for judgment to begin at the house of God; and if it begins with us first, what will be the end of those who do not obey the gospel of God? Now 'If the righteous one is scarcely saved, where will the ungodly and the sinner appear?'" What we see here is that the judgment of the surrounding nations was for much the same reason God judged Israel and Judah.

In particular with Moab, chapter 48 opens with a vivid description of the cities of Moab as they are overwhelmed one after another by the advance of the Babylonian army. See Moab was off the beaten track. No invading nation previously had gone out of their way to invade them. Because of that, the Moabites were smug, self-confident, and proud.

Yet judgment was coming on Moab and its chief false god (see v. 7). Look at verse 13: "'Moab shall be ashamed of Chemosh, as the house of Israel was ashamed of Bethel, their confidence.'" Now speaking of Bethel, this refers to the city in the northern tribe of Israel under the leadership of Jeroboam at the very beginning when the nation was divided. It was in Bethel Jeroboam set up a golden calf for the people to worship out of fear that if they went back to Jerusalem, which was in the southern kingdom, and worshipped there, they might defect to the southern kingdom. So he set up this golden calf there (and at Dan in the north), and it became Israel's center for idolatry. And God said, "Look, I judged the northern kingdom for idolatry, and I'm going to judge Moab as well."

One of the underlying principles I want us to see here is what this tells us about the authority and dominion of God. Is He the God of only the Jews? Was His power and authority restricted to those who recognized and claimed Him as their Sovereign? No, I think what we see from this passage of Scripture is He is the God of all creation. Colossians 1:15–17 speaks of Jesus like this: "He is the image of the invisible God, the firstborn over all creation. For by Him all things were created that are in heaven and that are on earth, visible and invisible, whether thrones or dominions or principalities or powers. All things were created through Him and for Him. And He is before all things, and in Him all things consist." God is the Creator. If we create something, we have control over it. And that's one of the reasons we've seen a rejection of the idea that God is Creator in the past one-hundred-plus years. Because if God is the Creator, then He can set the rules, which is exactly what He has done. And so God is the God of all creation.

Abraham spoke to God's authority. God called out Abraham. This was in the very beginning. And you might recall when Abraham had a kind of split from his nephew, Lot. Lot wanted the fertile plains, and he ended up in Sodom and Gomorrah, and God had come down to judge them because of their sexual immorality. And you may recall that Abraham interceded on behalf of Lot and his family, essentially saying, Hey, if there are one hundred righteous—and he got all the way down to ten—will you spare the city? And we read a part of his appeal over in Genesis 18:25: "Far be it from You to do such a thing as this, to slay the righteous with the wicked, so that the righteous should be as the wicked; far be it from You! Shall not the Judge of all the earth do right?" See, Abraham recognized God as the Judge of all Earth.

This next passage comes from Daniel's vision of the future. Looking into the future to Jesus and to His eventual reign, he said in Daniel 7:14, "Then to Him was given dominion and glory and a kingdom, that all peoples, nations, and languages should serve Him. His dominion is an everlasting dominion, which shall not pass away, and His kingdom the one which shall not be destroyed." See the Bible establishes God was not and is not a local deity or the God of only a nation. Rather, He is the ruler of nations. This, I believe, was communicated in these chapters to the children of Israel, Judah, for the benefit of God's people all around them. These other nations had their gods and the tendency to see that their gods had a geographical boundary. And when the children of Israel were carried off into captivity, because they had been worshipping idols and were so confused and spiritually perverted, they would think they had left their God behind. They were supposed to pray toward the temple, in which was the presence of God. When the temple was destroyed, they would have thought, *What hope is there?*

I think God was trying to show them He wasn't just the God over the nation, Israel and Judah; He was and is the God of all creation. All nations are held in account to Him. So I think it was a source of encouragement that, no matter where they were carried away, their God, Jehovah, was God. And that no matter where they went, they were not beyond the boundaries of His reach as they returned to Him. Still, they went to Jeremiah and said, "We will pray to God and ask for direction," knowing all along that they were going to go regardless. They were just looking for God to affirm the decision they had already made, and God warned them, "Don't go. You are looking for peace and prosperity. You're trying to avoid and run from destruction because of what had happened with Gedaliah." They were afraid that Nebuchadnezzar was going to come back upon them. God said, "Look, I'll take care of you. I will protect you. You will be OK here. Stay here. Trust me." Well, they decided to run anyway, and God said this, "Look, you can run, but what you're running from is going to find you."

You see, what we often run from in our own strength, we alternately run into and are consumed by because of our weakness. God told them to trust Him, and they would not. They ran to Egypt, and as God had prophesied through Jeremiah, Nebuchadnezzar went down to Egypt and destroyed it. Those who had lived through the destruction of Jerusalem and went to Egypt to find peace and prosperity found only more destruction and misery. See we can run, but we can't hide from God. Until we turn to God and stop running from Him, and accept by faith—meaning that we trust in Jesus Christ for the forgiveness of our sins—we stand condemned for our sin. And no matter where we go or what we try, there is no safe place out from under the protective hand of God.

Questions for Reflection and Discussion

1. Who was "Chemosh" of whom the Lord said Moab would be ashamed (see vv. 7, 13 then look at 1 Kings 11:33)?

2. After speaking of Moab's well-deserved disgrace and destruction, what words of hope did God give to Moab (v. 47)?

Notes on Today's Bible Reading

— DAY 38 —

Today's Reading: Jeremiah 49

Verse of the Day

> "For who is like Me? Who will arraign Me? And who is that shepherd who will withstand Me?"
>
> *Jeremiah 49:19b*

Please read the entire Scripture selection in your own Bible and highlight or underline verses that stand out to you before you read the observations and engage the questions below.

Just a reminder that chapters 46–51 are prophecies God gave Jeremiah against the surrounding nations. Jeremiah 49:19b reiterates the principle from the previous study that God is sovereign over all nations: "'For who is like Me? Who will arraign Me? And who is that shepherd who will withstand Me?" Remember, God punished Israel and Judah for their sin, then He systematically judged the other nations for their pride, idolatry, and wickedness. Again, recall 1 Peter 4:17 and the truth that judgment begins "at the house of God; and if it begins with us first, what will be the end of those who do not obey the gospel of God?" What we see here is the judgment of the surrounding nations was essentially for the same reasons God judged Israel and Judah.

Jeremiah 49 in particular begins with judgment pronounced on Ammon, an ancient enemy of God's people, in verses 1–6. Note that the god Milcom was identified as the Ammonites' chief state god

(v. 1). Yet Milcom and those who worship him went into captivity (v. 3). Next, judgment was pronounced on Edom, another enemy of God's people, in verses 7–22. Edom boasted of Petra, supposedly an impenetrable fortress. However, God declared in verse 10, "'But I have made Esau bare; I have uncovered his secret places, and he shall not be able to hide himself. His descendants are plundered, his brethren and his neighbors, and he is no more.'" In other words, the people of Edom could run, but they couldn't hide from God's judgment.

The next target was the ancient city of Damascus (vv. 23–27). Again, the Syrians were ancient foes of Israel. The Babylonian invasion would be devastating: "'Therefore her young men shall fall in her streets, and all the men of war shall be cut off in that day,' says the Lord of hosts. 'I will kindle a fire in the wall of Damascus, and it shall consume the palaces of Ben-Hadad'" (vv. 26–27) Then he turns to Kedar and Hazor in verses 28–33. These were likely Arab peoples. Kedar was more of a nomadic group. Hazor was more of a collection of villages. Neither lived in walled cities. Yet both groups would be swept aways by the Babylonian invasion: "'Hazor shall be a dwelling for jackals, a desolation forever; no one shall reside there, nor son of man dwell in it'" (v. 33).

Finally, in verses 34–36, God pronounced judgment on Elam, a reference to the people of Persia, or modern-day Iran. In the beginning, the Persians and Medes were allies of the Babylonians, but later they conquered the Babylonian Empire. However, God predicted their eventual conquest and fall, which occurred in history at the hand of the Greeks. One interesting note from verse 35 is that God declared, "'Behold, I will break the bow of Elam, the foremost of their might.'" In fact, Isaiah 22:6 refers to Elam's archers and their participation in the conquest of Jerusalem, where they served as allies to the Babylonians. But God promised a day when He would break the bow of Elam.

Again, don't get lost in the details and miss the primary principle from these pronouncements of judgment on various nations, kingdoms, and city-states. What does this tell us about God's sovereignty?

Is He only the God of the Jews? Is His power and authority limited to those who recognized and claimed Him as their God? Is He merely a local deity or the God of just the Jewish people or the nation of Israel? No. He is the God of *all* the nations. As we saw last time, God is the Creator, and if we create something, we are sovereign over it. Consequently, God is the Ruler of all creation, including all nations, and all are therefore accountable to Him—all will answer to Him. God makes this point repeatedly in these chapters. These other nations had their gods, and there was this tendency to see their gods as having a geographical boundary, but Yahweh does not have such a limitation. He is the Sovereign over all.

One additional principle is, while God pronounced judgment on each of these nations, there are some occasional glimmers of hope. At the end of section of judgment on the first and last nations of Ammon and Elam, there is a repeated refrain about a return to their land: "'But afterward I will bring back the captives of the people of Ammon" (39:6), and "'it shall come to pass in the latter days: I will bring back the captives of Elam,' says the Lord" (v. 39). To Edom there is God's offer: "'Leave your fatherless children, I will preserve them alive; and let your widows trust in Me'" (v. 11). God calls the ancient city of Damascus "'the city of My joy'" and promised it would not be completely deserted after the Babylonian invasion, as would be the case of other major cities of surrounding nations (v. 25). The message is that holy God must punish sin, but He also has a heart for people—all people in all nations. Indeed, God said in Ezekiel 33:11: "'I have no pleasure in the death of the wicked, but that the wicked turn from his way and live.'" Indeed, remember how Peter put it: "The Lord is . . . longsuffering [patient] toward us, not willing [desiring] that any should perish but that all should come to repentance" (2 Peter 3:9). It is also a reminder not to presume on God's grace, but to pray that the people of America will return to the Lord before His judgment becomes final on our nation.

Questions for Reflection and Discussion

1. Jeremiah followed his pronouncement of God's judgment with the promise that God would restore which of these nations in the latter days?

   a. Ammon
   b. Damascus
   c. Elam
   d. All of the above

2. Which kingdom was compared to Sodom and Gomorrah in its impending destruction?

Notes on Today's Bible Reading

— DAY 39 —

Today's Reading: Jeremiah 50–51

Verse of the Day

> "Behold, I am against you, O most haughty one!" says the Lord GOD of hosts; "for your day has come, the time that I will punish you."
>
> *Jeremiah 50:31*

Please read the entire Scripture selection in your own Bible and highlight or underline verses that stand out to you before you read the observations and engage the questions below.

Today we are going to talk about God's judgment on Babylon in chapters 50–51. Specifically, we will see why Babylon lost its status as the most powerful city in all the world and why it matters. Remember during the time of Jeremiah, Nebuchadnezzar ascended to the throne of the Babylonian Empire, taking over from his father. Under Nebuchadnezzar, Babylon became the leading empire of the entire world at the time. And the city itself, Babylon, became the greatest city in all the world. In fact, it was the site of one of the seven wonders of the ancient world, the hanging gardens. But as we saw in the last few studies, covering chapters 46–49, God, Yahweh, is Lord over all of creation. In fact, we see a reference to that even in our reading passage today. Jeremiah 51:15 says, "He has made the earth by His power; He has established the world by His wisdom, and stretched out the heaven by His understanding." And as the Creator, that means God, not humans, is the ultimate authority both for individuals and for nations. If there's one thing we've seen in these last few chapters, it is the sovereignty of God over individuals and over nations. God is the Lord. And keep that in mind because we're going to see that even more pronounced in the passages we read today and tomorrow.

Now we're going to answer three key questions in these chapters: (1) Why did God judge Babylon? (2) What was the punishment? (3) Why does it matter? So let's begin reading in Jeremiah 50:1–2: "The word that the LORD spoke against Babylon and against the land of the Chaldeans by Jeremiah the prophet. 'Declare among the nations, proclaim, and set up a standard; proclaim—do not conceal it—say, "Babylon is taken, Bel is shamed. Merodach is broken in pieces; her idols are humiliated, her images are broken in pieces." For out of the north a nation comes up against her, which shall make her land desolate, and no one shall dwell therein. They shall move, they shall depart, both man and beast.'" So these first three verses really provide insight into our first two questions. Why did God Judge Babylon? Well, let me ask you this: Why did he judge Israel? Why did he judge Judah? Why did he judge all of these other nations we read about in chapters 46–49? Remember, God has the same standard for everyone, for every nation. He is the same yesterday, today, and forever. Their idolatry and their pride were central to their downfall. Clearly, there was more to it and we'll look at it, but at the root was their idolatry and their pride.

Look at what Jeremiah 50:35 says: "'A sword is against the Chaldeans,' says the LORD, 'against the inhabitants of Babylon, and against her princes and her wise men.'" The next few verses list all the offenders and the targets of God's wrath. And then they tell us why. First look at Jeremiah 50:38: "'A drought is against her waters, and they will be dried up. For it is the land of carved images, and they are insane with their idols.'" Look at Jeremiah 51:17–18: "Everyone is dull-hearted, without knowledge; every metalsmith is put to shame by the carved image; for his molded image is falsehood, and there is no breath in them. They are futile, a work of errors; in the time of their punishment they shall perish." And also read Jeremiah 51:47: "'Therefore behold, the days are coming that I will bring judgment on the carved images of Babylon; her whole land shall be ashamed, and all her slain shall fall in her midst.'" There are more reasons for God's judgment, which I will get to, but I want to park on this one for just a moment.

I want to take us back to the Ten Commandments and look at the very first from Exodus 20:3: "'You shall have no other gods before Me,'" meaning nothing should take preeminence over the Creator, over God. And then in 20:4–5, "'You shall not make for yourself a carved image . . . ; you shall not bow down to them nor serve them.'" In short, we are not to serve the works of our own hands. Why were these the first two of the ten? Well, I submit to you the reason is, if you get this wrong, you're going to end up in the wrong place. You've blown it.

The one true God must take preeminence in our lives. God cannot be an addendum to our lives. He cannot be an accessory to our lives. He must be central. And that's true for us as followers of Jesus Christ today. Jesus, the Word of God Himself, must be central to our lives. He must be preeminent, and by extension, that should be true in our nation if we want the blessing of God. As it was recorded in Acts 17:28, Paul said this: "in Him we live and move and have our being." He should be central to everything. And if that's not the case in your life, you need to spend some time in the presence of God, and you need to make Him central, the core of who you are. Lastly, you follow the path of others in history and nations. And again, God is the same yesterday, today, and forever.

Now from this idolatry and pride, we see the other sins that led to the judgment of Babylon in Jeremiah 50:7: "'All who found them have devoured them; and their adversaries said, "We have not offended, because they have sinned against the LORD, the habitation of justice, the LORD, the hope of their fathers."'" God used Babylon to judge Judah. We read this not only in Jeremiah, but if we go back to Isaiah, this was predicted two hundred years previously; this would occur even before Babylon was an entity to be considered. Even though God used them, God held them accountable. They said, "Oh, we can take care of these people because they sinned against their God." Well, we need to be careful about that. These nations that God used to judge His people will themselves be judged. Look at Jeremiah 50:15, "'Shout against her all around; she has given her hand, her foundations have fallen, her walls are thrown down; for it is the vengeance of the LORD. Take vengeance on her. As she has done, so do to her.'" Remember, "Vengeance is mine," says the Lord, and He's doing this on behalf of His people because of what they did to Judah and Israel.

Look at Jeremiah 50:18: "Therefore thus says the LORD of hosts, the God of Israel: 'Behold, I will punish the king of Babylon and his land, as I have punished the king of Assyria.'" Now jump to verse 24: "'I have laid a snare for you; you have indeed been trapped, O Babylon, and you were not aware; you have been found and also caught, because you have contended against the LORD.'" They opposed the Lord and his purposes. Now look at verse 29: "'Call together the archers against Babylon. All you who bend the bow, encamp against it all around; let none of them escape. Repay her according to her work; according to all she has done, do to her; for she has been proud against the LORD, against the Holy One of Israel.'" Again, this is a nation that had their own gods, but God was holding them accountable for the pride they had and the fact that they defied the one true living God. Jeremiah 50:31 says, "'Behold, I am against you, O most haughty one!' says the LORD God of hosts; 'for your day has come, the time that I will punish you.'" And Jeremiah 51:11 says, "Make the arrows bright! Gather the shields! The LORD has raised up the spirit of the kings of the Medes. For His plan is against Babylon to destroy it, because it is the vengeance of the LORD, the vengeance for His temple." Remember, they destroyed the temple. They took vengeance on the people. They abused the people. And the Lord says, I'm taking vengeance for this.

Moving on, let's read Jeremiah 51:13: "O you who dwell by many waters, abundant in treasures, your end has come, the measure of your covetousness." This was speaking to their prosperity, and there was a lot of covetousness. They were consumers. There's a warning! Now jump over to verse 35: "'Let the violence done to me and my flesh be upon Babylon,' the inhabitant of Zion will say; 'And my blood be upon the inhabitants of Chaldea!' Jerusalem will say." And then verse 56: "Because the plunderer comes against her, against Babylon, and her mighty men are taken. Every one of their bows is broken; for the LORD is the God of recompense, He will surely repay." See, what they had done was coming back on them. Their idolatry and pride was at the core of charting their course of destruction. We see it manifesting in the way they treated others—the fact they defied God and saw themselves above God—and God ultimately brought the most powerful nation and all the world down to rubble.

What was the punishment and why does it matter? In a nutshell, desolation, utter destruction to the point no one would ever inhabit the city again. Let's look at the verses from these two chapters that speak to this: Specifically,

- 50:13: "'Because of the wrath of the LORD she shall not be inhabited, but she shall be wholly desolate. Everyone who goes by Babylon shall be horrified and hiss at all her plagues.'"
- 50:34: "'Their Redeemer is strong; the LORD of hosts is His name. He will thoroughly plead their case, that He may give rest to the land, and disquiet the inhabitants of Babylon.'"
- 50:39: "'Therefore the wild desert beasts shall dwell there with the jackals, and the ostriches shall dwell in it. It shall be inhabited no more forever, nor shall it be dwelt in from generation to generation.'"
- 51:29: "And the land will tremble and sorrow; for every purpose of the LORD shall be performed against Babylon, to make the land of Babylon a desolation without inhabitant."
- 51:37: "'Babylon shall become a heap, a dwelling place for jackals, an astonishment and a hissing, without an inhabitant.'"
- 51:43: "'Her cities are a desolation, a dry land and a wilderness, a land where no one dwells, through which no son of man passes.'"
- 51:62: "'[T]hen you shall say, 'O LORD, You have spoken against this place to cut it off, so that none shall remain in it, neither man nor beast, but it shall be desolate forever.'"

Jeremiah's prophecy, as we mentioned earlier, came probably three to five years after the destruction of Jerusalem but well before the destruction of Babylon. Isaiah predicted the same outcome nearly two hundred years before, when Babylon as of yet was not even a world power. And look back at Isaiah 13:19: "'And Babylon, the glory of kingdoms, the beauty of the Chaldeans' pride, will be as when God overthrew Sodom and Gomorrah.'" It is amazing how Sodom and Gomorrah is kind of the benchmark of God's judgment. We see this throughout Scripture. It's mentioned in the Old Testament and the New Testament. We see this reference to Sodom and Gomorrah as a judgment of God, which was definitive. And people don't want to acknowledge it, but it was because of the sexual immorality that took place in Sodom and Gomorrah.

Now look at Isaiah 13:20–22: "'It will never be inhabited, nor will it be settled from generation to generation; nor will the Arabian pitch tents there, nor will the shepherds make their sheepfolds there. But wild beasts of the desert will lie there, and their houses will be full of owls; ostriches will dwell there, and wild goats will caper there. The hyenas will howl in their citadels, and jackals in their pleasant palaces. Her time is near to come, and her days will not be prolonged.'" This prophecy is yet more evidence of the veracity of the truth of Scripture. Fully 2,500 years after the destruction of Babylon, this Word of God is still being fulfilled. To this day, Babylon remains uninhabited—not that men have not tried to rebuild the city and inhabit it. In fact, in 1987, it was completed. Saddam Hussein rebuilt the city of Babylon. He built these elaborate palaces for himself and the city walls and all of these other things around there. But it was never inhabited. Remember the war? Today even, despite this elaborate building project that siphoned off resources from the Iraqi people, the city remains a haunt of wild animals. Pretty amazing.

Well, that brings us to our final point: Why does it matter? (1) God's Word is true. "It will not return unto him void without effect." His Word will accomplish what He declares. (2) God judged nations for their idolatry and their pride. No nation was exempt. From Israel, His covenant people, to Babylon, the nation that He used to judge Israel and Judah and the other nations. No nation got a pass.

Now this should be a wake-up call for America. Because of our idolatry, our nation is dancing dangerously on the precipice of God's judgment. We don't have stoned images or carved images we bow down to, but we do worship the work of our hands, and we have placed things before God. We need to do an inventory, and we need to be praying and interceding for this nation. I believe America is in trouble.

Finally (3): God does not forsake His children. This is where we find encouragement. Jeremiah 51:5–6 says, "'For Israel is not forsaken, nor Judah, by his God, the LORD of hosts, though their land was filled with sin against the Holy One of Israel.' Flee from the midst of Babylon, and every one save his life! Do not be cut off in her iniquity, for this is the time of the LORD's vengeance; He shall recompense her." We need to be praying and working to see the church as a searchlight to the nations, beginning right here in the United States. But despite the circumstances we now see—which I believe are going to get worse as we move further and further away from the truth of God's Word as a nation, culturally or politically—we can stand on this promise. This doesn't mean we are immune to the effects or we should be silent. But we can stand with confidence and firmness on the promise God will not forsake His children.

Because we hear this all the time, especially politicians saying, "We're all God's children," I want to focus on that for a moment. I hate to say it, but we're not all God's children. We're all God's creation, but we only become His children when we're adopted into His family, and we're adopted into the family of God when we accept Jesus Christ as our Savior and our Lord. Then we become children of God. And when we're children of God, we have this promise that He will not forsake, as He will never leave us nor forsake us. When we look at Babylon, it is the world's system, and ultimately judgment is going to come upon this world system. But here's the promise that God will not forsake His children. And so while we are in this world, we must, as He told the children of Israel, flee from the midst of Babylon, spiritually; I believe we need to flee the Babylon of this age, the world system. I'm not talking about going off the grid. I'm talking about what it says in Romans 12:2: "And do not be conformed to this world, but be transformed by the renewing of your mind, that you may prove what is that good and acceptable and perfect will of God." You see, we do not need to be part of the world system, so absorbed into it that we lose focus and we lose purpose and we lose the hope we have that God will not forsake His children. When God's judgment comes upon this world, and it will, we will be delivered by the grace of God, and that's true each and every day as our minds are transformed. Again, we're not talking about running away. I'm talking about living with a mind that is renewed in Christ with our focus upon Him. And His promises are true.

Questions for Reflection and Discussion

1. What did Jeremiah tell us about Israel's Redeemer (see 50:34)?

2. What were the Babylonians failing to take into account about God's relationship with His people (see v. 5)?

Notes on Today's Bible Reading

— DAY 40 —

Today's Reading: Jeremiah 52

Verse of the Day

> He also put out the eyes of Zedekiah; and the king of Babylon bound him in bronze fetters, took him to Babylon, and put him in prison till the day of his death.
>
> *Jeremiah 52:11*

Please read the entire Scripture selection in your own Bible and highlight or underline verses that stand out to you before you read the observations and engage the questions below.

With a look at chapter 52, we come to the end of our forty-day journey through the book of Jeremiah. Today our key verse is 11, which reads, "He also put out the eyes of Zedekiah; and the king of Babylon bound him in bronze fetters, took him to Babylon, and put him in prison till the day of his death." This chapter is basically a historical supplement on the final invasion of Jerusalem by Nebuchadnezzar in 587–86 BC. This historical account, which was probably added by Ezra, is essentially the same thing we see in 2 Kings 25, which was written by Jeremiah. What is added is the disposition of Zedekiah, what happened after he was carried away into captivity. But I want us to focus on the fact history proves the prophecies of God to be true. And that's what we see from this account. Let's look at a couple of thoughts from Jeremiah's concluding chapter.

Let's start in verses 1–11.

Zedekiah was twenty-one years old when he became king, and he reigned eleven years in Jerusalem. His mother's name was Hamutal the daughter of Jeremiah of Libnah. He also did evil in the sight of the Lord, according to all that Jehoiakim had done. For because of the anger of the Lord this happened in Jerusalem and Judah, till He finally cast them out from His presence. Then Zedekiah rebelled against the king of Babylon. Now it came to pass in the ninth year of his reign, in the tenth month, on the tenth day of the month, that Nebuchadnezzar king of Babylon and all his army came against Jerusalem and encamped against it; and they built a siege wall against it all around. So the city was besieged until the eleventh year of King Zedekiah. By the fourth month, on the ninth day of the month, the famine had become so severe in the city that there was no food for the people of the land. Then the city wall was broken through, and all the men of war fled and went out of the city at night by way of the gate between the two walls, which was by the king's garden, even though the Chaldeans were near the city all around. And they went by way of the plain. But the army of the Chaldeans pursued the king, and they overtook Zedekiah in the plains of Jericho. All his army was scattered from him. So they took the king and brought him up to the king of Babylon at Riblah in the land of Hamath, and he pronounced judgment on him. Then the king of Babylon killed the sons of Zedekiah before his eyes. And he killed all the princes of Judah in Riblah. He also put out the eyes of Zedekiah; and the king of Babylon bound him in bronze fetters, took him to Babylon, and put him in prison till the day of his death.

Now recall, Zedekiah could have avoided all of this. Back in chapter 38, Jeremiah warned him to surrender and not rebel. Yet he rebelled against God. Remember that Judah, Jerusalem, was under tribute to Babylon. That's why Nebuchadnezzar was coming back again; they kept rebelling and refusing to submit to Babylon. And so, if we don't submit to God, we're going to have to submit to tyrants. And if the nation refused to serve God and Babylon came in, but they refused to serve Babylon, God was going to destroy them because that was part of their punishment. Take a look back at Jeremiah 38:17–20.

> Then Jeremiah said to Zedekiah, "Thus says the Lord, the God of hosts, the God of Israel: 'If you surely surrender to the king of Babylon's princes, then your soul shall live; this city shall not be burned with fire, and you and your house shall live. But if you do not surrender to the king of Babylon's princes, then this city shall be given into the hand of the Chaldeans; they shall burn it with fire, and you shall not escape from their hand.'" And Zedekiah the king said to Jeremiah, "I am afraid of the Jews who have defected to the Chaldeans, lest they deliver me into their hand, and they abuse me." But Jeremiah said, "They shall not deliver you. Please, obey the voice of the Lord which I speak to you. So it shall be well with you, and your soul shall live."

Now remember, everything Jeremiah had prophesied was coming about. He prophesied this moment was coming where the city was again going to be under siege by the Chaldeans ruled by Nebuchadnezzar. All this was unfolding. Everything Jeremiah had said was true, and so here he is, once again, finally laying this out before Zedekiah: "Surrender, submit, and it will be well with you." Zedekiah said he's afraid to do it. So in verses 21–23, Jeremiah says,

> "But if you refuse to surrender, this is the word that the Lord has shown me: 'Now behold, all the women who are left in the king of Judah's house shall be surrendered to the king of Babylon's princes, and those women shall say: "Your close friends have set upon you and prevailed against you; your feet have sunk in the mire, and they have turned away again." So they shall surrender all your wives and children to the Chaldeans.

> You shall not escape from their hand, but shall be taken by the hand of the king of Babylon. And you shall cause this city to be burned with fire.'"

"Here's the option," he said. "You submit, your family, the city, the temple will all be spared. You don't, and your family is going to be carried out, the city is going to be burned, the temple will be destroyed." So Zedekiah continued in his rebellion against God and Nebuchadnezzar. The result was everything that they were trusting in, they had hoped in, was destroyed. Number one, religion. They had this idea that the presence of God's temple in Jerusalem and the fact they were "God's people" was going to preserve them. They were wrong.

Remember Jeremiah 7:4, where He says, "'Do not trust in these lying words, saying, "The temple of the LORD, the temple of the LORD, the temple of the LORD are these."'" This was hearkening back to the day of Hezekiah, when Sennacherib was surrounding the city and Hezekiah repented. He prayed to God. And as a result, the army of Sennacherib was miraculously decimated by one of God's angelic warriors, the Assyrians were forced to withdraw, and the city was spared. And they attributed that to the fact the temple was there, God's presence was there, but they were just relying on religion, not a relationship.

We have to be very careful that we're not relying upon religion or we're a Christian nation or we go to church. First off, when we're believers, we must realize we're in a spiritual war, so opposition is going to come. That's the reason Paul wrote in Ephesians 6 that we must put on the full armor of God. We've got to be engaging in a relationship with God—putting on the breastplate of righteousness, the belt of truth, the helmet of salvation; having our feet shod with the preparation of the gospel of faith; taking up the shield of faith and the sword of the Spirit, which is the Word of God. You don't do that just by being in a religion. It's through a relationship with Jesus Christ.

So they were counting on religion and what happened? They lost it. They were counting on their security. They were in a fortified city. Jerusalem was on a hill, on a mountain. And they had high walls so nothing could get them. They thought they were invincible. But

Psalm 20:7 says, "Some trust in chariots, and some in horses; but we will remember the name of the LORD our God." Strong military fortifications, while they're essential, are not the final defense we need. They're not going to protect us when God is against us. It doesn't matter what we have on our side. What we need is God, and what that requires is—as an individual, as a nation—we're walking in obedience to God. Then third and finally, the people were prosperous. What is a kingdom without people? All of that was gone. We read that by the end of the siege there was no food in the city. They were starving. They were literally eating one another. It was a desperate situation. And so they lost everything, the religion, the security, the people.

Now, let's pick back up in Jeremiah 52:12–15.

> Now in the fifth month, on the tenth day of the month (which was the nineteenth year of King Nebuchadnezzar king of Babylon), Nebuzaradan, the captain of the guard, who served the king of Babylon, came to Jerusalem. He burned the house of the LORD and the king's house; all the houses of Jerusalem, that is, all the houses of the great, he burned with fire. And all the army of the Chaldeans who were with the captain of the guard broke down all the walls of Jerusalem all around. Then Nebuzaradan the captain of the guard carried away captive some of the poor people, the rest of the people who remained in the city, the defectors who had deserted to the king of Babylon, and the rest of the craftsmen.

Here's the final thought on this: Rebellion toward God comes at a high, high price, both for individuals and nations. God has made quite clear in His Word that we are to submit to Him; we are to surrender to Him, to confess our sins, receive forgiveness for our sins, and walk in obedience before Him.

God's grace, as we see here in the book of Jeremiah, is so long-suffering because He wants people and nations to turn back to Him. But there comes a point where chastisement, punishment, and judgment comes. What is that point? Well, we don't always know, but this we do know: what He has said will occur. And so it is in our best interest, as it was for Zedekiah, to submit to God and cease the rebellion because ultimately it was the rebellion of Zedekiah that led to his complete and total blindness. He was blinded to the truth, and he decided he wanted to walk in that blindness. Well, what we see at the very end is that his eyes were put out after the last thing he saw was his own sons, his own family murdered before him. And then his eyes were taken out, and he was held captive in prison for the rest of his life. So we can be set free if we choose to walk in the light and choose the truth. We can have that freedom, and we can see clearly. And so my prayer for you as we conclude this journey is that you are walking in the light, free from the bondage of sin and death, which comes upon us in our natural state. It's all a matter of just trusting in the Lord Jesus Christ, asking Him to be your Lord and Savior, and placing your faith in Him—and by God's grace, walking in the freedom that comes then being obedient and walking in obedience before God. Like Jeremiah, the prophet they could not cancel, take your stand and speak God's Word courageously and winsomely to a world that needs to be set free. May God bless you as you do.

Questions for Reflection and Discussion

1. What did the Babylonians do once they defeated the remainder of the Judean army, executed King Zedekiah's sons, and took him into captivity (see vv. 12–27)?

   a. Burned the temple
   b. Burned the king's palace
   c. Broke down all the walls around Jerusalem
   d. Brought most of the survivors into captivity
   e. All of the above

2. What did King Nebuchadnezzar do with the rest of the leaders who remained in the city of Jerusalem after the siege (see vv. 24–27)?

Notes on Today's Bible Reading

— APPENDIX 1 —

Stand on the Word Bible Reading Plan

Visit frc.org/Bible for our chronological journey through the Bible that we call "Stand on the Word." We encourage you to spend time reading and studying the Bible because it is literally "God-breathed" (see 2 Tim. 3:16); it is God's very words to us. The Bible answers the big questions, such as, Why am I here? Where did I come from? Where am I going (life after death)? If God is good, why does evil and suffering exist? The Bible not only answers these big questions; it offers practical advice in areas such as, How can I deal with feelings of fear or anger or guilt? How can I forgive when I cannot forget? What should I look for in a spouse? How can I have a successful marriage? How can I be a good parent? What is my spiritual gift and place in the church? What is my stewardship responsibility as a citizen? We learned the verse in Bible School, "Your word is a lamp to my feet and a light to my path" (Ps. 119:105). God's Word shows us the way forward in any area of life and on every question we face.

The Stand on the Word Bible Reading Plan takes us through the Bible chronologically. In other words, each reading takes you through the Bible as events occurred in history as far as it is possible. Here is how it works for our family. At the same time each morning, whether I am at home, in Washington, or some foreign country, I send my wife and children a morning greeting along with a reminder of the passage for the day. The text includes two questions related to the reading.

The questions are designed to help in content retention, serve as an accountability tool, and provide for discussion.

The two-year plan does not have a Sunday passage. Instead, it provides an outline for a family discussion that can be done on Sunday afternoon or evening each week. The weekly discussion time begins with a spiritual leader asking each person individually for one or two insights or truths they gained from their reading during the week. After everyone else shares, you can then lead a short discussion based upon one of the passages that you read in the week just completed. It is also a time for them to ask questions.

By the way, you don't have to have all the answers. If you don't know, tell them so, then talk to your pastor or other trusted person with Bible knowledge. If your children start asking questions, that suggests they are thinking about what they are reading.

Reading God's Word will help you establish a fruitful walk with the God who made you and loves you. Whether you are single or married, this plan will enable you to lead your friends and family in daily reading God's Word. The added benefit is that you will all be reading the same text together. It will amaze you to see how God speaks sometimes in the same ways and at other times in different ways to each of you. Being on this journey together will build a spiritual synergy, a deep bond and sense of unity and purpose like nothing else! Use it to impart the Word of life.

— APPENDIX 2 —

Prayer: Talking with God

Most Americans say they pray. But not as many pray the way Jesus did, the way He taught His disciples to pray. Fewer, still, really know the power in prayer God gave us to impact our families, communities, nation, and world. Prayer is our lifeline to God, our means of communicating with our heavenly Father. It develops our relationship—our friendship, fellowship, and intimacy with Him. In prayer we experience God and are "filled with the Spirit" (see Eph. 5:18–21). God uses the prayers of faithful men, women, boys, and girls to heal broken lives and strengthen families, churches, communities, and even nations. He uses our prayers to advance his Kingdom on earth (Daniel 9; Acts 4:36). He wants to use all believers!

The Essence of Prayer

Prayer is simply talking with God—about anything and everything. He is our Maker, Father, Savior, Provider, and Counselor; our Master, Healer, Guide, and Friend. Christ died for our sins and rose from the dead to sit at the right hand of God the Father, where He is praying for us *right now* (Heb. 10:12). His Spirit now lives within us and helps us to pray (1 John 4:16).

The Priority of Prayer

Jesus spent time alone with God regularly drawing strength from the Father and seeking His will for every decision (Luke 6:12–13;

22:39–44). His disciples asked Jesus to teach them how to pray (Luke 11:1–13). The apostles knew that prayer and obedience were the keys to Christ's life and ministry and were determined to follow His example: "[W]e will give ourselves to prayer and to the ministry of the word" (Acts 6:4). Too few American men pray today, even pastors and leaders! Yet strong praying men are the norm in Scripture. Our families, churches, and nation need men who will make prayer a priority today! (1 Tim. 2:8)

The Practice of Prayer

Scripture teaches, "Pray without ceasing" (1 Thess. 5:17); "Praying always" (Eph. 6:18); "Always . . . pray and not lose heart" (Luke 18:1). Below are some helps to get you started. No one can beat the Lord's Prayer. It is an outline of key themes to guide our prayer lives: "'Our Father in heaven, hallowed be Your name. Your kingdom come. Your will be done on earth as it is in heaven. Give us this day our daily bread. And forgive us our debts, as we forgive our debtors. And do not lead us into temptation, but deliver us from the evil one" (Matt. 6:9–13a).

In the book of Psalms and throughout Scripture, God has sprinkled prayers/patterns for us to learn from. Here is a simple, popular acronym to help jog our memories:

P-R-A-Y:

- *Praise:* Our Father which art in heaven, hallowed be thy name.
- *Repent:* And forgive us our debts, as we forgive our debtors.
- *Ask:* Give us this day our daily bread. And forgive us our debts, as we forgive our debtors. And lead us not into temptation but deliver us from evil.
- *Yield:* Thy kingdom come. Thy will be done in earth, as it is in heaven.

Praying through Scripture

God also talks to us. The Bible is His Word (2 Tim. 2:15; 3:16). Bible in hand, we should pray God's promises back to Him and claim them for our families, our work, our finances, and our nation (1 Tim.2:1–8; 1 John 5:14–15).

Scriptures to Pray as a Man: Joshua 1:8; 1 Timothy 3:1–15; 1 Chronicles 12:32; 1 Timothy 6:1–12; 1 Corinthians 16:13; Romans 12:1–21; Micah 6:8; John 4:24; Acts 2:38: 1 Kings 2:2; ***Husbands***: Ephesians 5:25–28; Genesis 2:24;1 Peter 3:7; Ephesians 4:26–27; Matthew 5:32; Proverbs 5:19; 1 Corinthians 6:18; ***Fathers***: Deuteronomy 4:8–10; 11:18–21; Exodus 34:5–8; Psalm 127:3–5; Matthew 7:11; Ephesians 6:4; Proverbs 22:6; Luke 11:11–12; Hebrews 12:5–7

Scriptures to Pray as a Woman: Matthew 22:36–40; Proverbs 31:30; 1 Peter 3:1–3; Ephesians 5:26; Ephesians 4:15, 29; 1 Timothy 3:11; Ephesians 5:22, 24; 1 Peter 3:1–2; Philippians 4:10– 13; Philippians 2:3–4; Proverbs 31:12; 1 Corinthians 7:34; Titus 2:3– 4; Titus 2:4–5; James 1:19; Ephesians 4:32; 1 Corinthians 7:1–5; Luke 2:37; Colossians 4:2; Proverbs 31:27; 1 Timothy 5:14; 1 Timothy 5:14

Scriptures to Pray for Your Children: Matthew 22:36–40; 2 Timothy 3:15; Psalm 97:10, 38:18; Proverbs 8:13; John 17:15, 10:10; Romans 12:9; Psalm 119:71; Hebrews 12:5–6; Daniel 1:17, 20; Proverbs 1:4; James 1:5; Romans 13:1; Ephesians 6:1–3; Hebrews 13:17; Proverbs 1:10–16; 13:20; 2 Corinthians 6:14–17; Deuteronomy 6; 1 Corinthians 6:18–20; Acts 24:16; 1 Timothy 1:19, 4:1–2; Titus 1:15–16; Psalm 23:4; Deuteronomy 10:12; Matthew 28:18–20; Ephesians 1:3, 4:29; Ephesians 1:16–19; Philippians 1:11; Colossians 1:9; Philippians 1:9–10

Developing Personal Prayer Habits

Rise early each day to pray with opened Bible. Daniel prayed three times daily. Pray whenever you can: as you drive, with your wife, with your children at dinner and before bedtime. You cannot pray too much!

Praying Together with Others

Pray with your spouse regularly. Make time for family prayer. Be part of your church prayer meeting or group. Christ said, "'My house shall be called a house of prayer'" (Matt. 21:13). The apostle Paul instructed Pastor Timothy to make prayer the first order of the church, saying prayer is key to peace in the nation (1 Tim. 2:1–8). There is nothing like a Spirit-led prayer meeting with people who love the Lord! Praying women have been standing in the prayer gap for decades. Every man must set his heart to become a praying man, lead his family in prayer, and be a strong contributor to the corporate prayer life of his church. We must be leaders in praying for our morally and spiritually troubled, divided nation—and for our national leaders. American Christians simply must respond to God's promise: "[I]f My people who are called by My name will humble themselves, and pray and seek My face, and turn from their wicked ways, then I will hear from heaven, and will forgive their sin and heal their land" (2 Chron. 7:14).

Prayer As Warfare

Jesus described the enemy, the devil, as a thief whose mission is to "steal, and to kill, and to destroy" (John 10:10). Demonic forces are at war against everything good in you, your family, your church, your community, America, and every nation (Ephesians 6:10–20).

The devil and his minions are out to thwart the kingdom of God and eliminate righteousness wherever he can. He hates God and hates people and will use spiritually ignorant and deceived men, women, boys, and girls to do his bidding. Men of God today, like the sons of Issachar in ancient Israel, need to understand the times and know what the church and our nation must do (1 Chron. 12:32). We must pull down Satan's strongholds, wrestle for our families, and use Spirit-led prayer and wisdom to help guide our churches and communities to prevail against the evil onslaught against us (2 Cor. 10:3–5). This is the war of the ages, and it is real.

Finally, Determine to Become a Person of Prayer

No matter how long you have been a Christian and may have neglected prayer up until now, you can become a person of prayer starting today. If you have missed the mark, it is not too late. Call upon the Lord, ask for His help, and proceed with His guidance. O Lord, make me a praying person; make me a prayer warrior! In Jesus's name, amen!

Notes

1. Dietrich Bonhoeffer, *The Cost of Discipleship* (New York: Macmillan, 1963), 47.

2. Matthew Henry, *An Exposition of the Old and New Testament: Wherein Each Chapter Is Summed Up in Its Contents*, 6 vols. (London: Henry G. Bohn, 1753), 4:320.

3. Ibid.

4. Ashley Kirzinger et al., "Public Knowledge and Attitudes About Sexually Transmitted Infections: KFF Polling and Policy Insights," kff.org, February 18, 2020, https://www.kff.org/womens-health-policy/issue-brief/public-knowledge-and-attitudes-about-sexually-transmitted-infections/.

5. William Penn, *Frame of Government of Pennsylvania*, May 5, 1682 as found at https://avalon.law.yale.edu/17th_century/pa04.asp (Yale Law School Avalon Project).

6. https://www.jec.senate.gov/public/index.cfm/republicans/2020/4/marriage-rate-blog-test

7. W. Bradford Wilcox, "Married Parents: One Way to Reduce Child Poverty," Institute for Family Studies, June 21, 2017, https://ifstudies.org/blog/married-parents-one-way-to-reduce-child-poverty.

8. William Bradford, *History of Plymouth Plantation 1620–1647*, ed. William Chauncey Ford, 2 vols. (Boston: Massachusetts Historical Society, 1912), 1:55.

9. Henry, *An Exposition*, 4:413–14.

10. While the comparison of Max Jukes and Jonathan Edwards is found multiple places online, the original source is the research done in Richard Dugdale, "The Jukes: A Study of Crime, Pauperism, Disease and Heredity" (1969). *Buck v. Bell Documents*, paper 1, http://readingroom.law.gsu.edu/buckvbell/1. Dr. Rick Fricks does some myth busting of certain details of the story, but the gist of it holds up to scrutiny; see http://rfrick.info/jukes.htm.

11. "Rep. Jerry Nadler: 'What Any Religious Tradition Ascribes as God's Will is No Concern of This Congress,'" cnsnews.com, March 1, 2021, https://www.cnsnews.com/article/washington/cnsnewscom-staff/rep-jerry-nadler-what-any-religious-tradition-ascribes-gods

12. Henry, *An Exposition*, 4:349.

13. Henry, *An Exposition*, 4:250.